ROOFTOP SOLAR SECRETS

The Ultimate Guide To Going Solar

NICK GORDEN

Shine Solar, LLC

Find us on Facebook at facebook.com/Shinesolarpower,
visit our website at www.shinesolar.com, or
call us at 1-844-80-SHINE.

Shine Solar Customer Testimonials

"Going solar isn't as difficult as one may think. In fact, it is easily done with one call to Shine Solar. They offer a turnkey installation that is second to none! My wife and I now have a 5.6Kw system. The hardest part of the whole process for us was waiting to 'flip the switch!' . . . we couldn't be more satisfied with their service!"

Seth M.

". . . This is something I have wanted to do but thought it was beyond my means. Very responsive to questions at any time."

Catherine R.

"I love having solar! It's so fun going out and watching my meter move backwards, producing more energy than I'm using."

Sage O.

"It pays for itself, and the Shine Solar process was efficient and easy. We put forth no effort on our end, and the installation crew was easy to get along with. With energy costs rising, what you save in utility bills pays for the monthly payment, plus it's great for the environment. The panels convert energy from one source to another with no effort!"

Ken H.

"It was a quick and easy process. We were able to reduce our footprint while we save money. The benefit is that our electric bill, which is $600 in the winter, will be much less.

Lee O.

"The experience was easy and the excitement around how innovating it is was so fun! I love watching my meter go backwards. You can do 2, 10 or 20 panels. It all depends on what you can afford over the long term and how long you plan on living in the house. The install team was polite and friendly!"

Greg E.

"Great company!! Down to earth, hard working, honest people motivated to benefit customers"

Trish & Ott B.

"I really appreciate what you guys did and it's just an absolute gorgeous, gorgeous system and I am so excited to see that meter spin backwards, I really am. When I saw the flexibility of not having to outlay so much cash up-front, I've been able to work that a little bit more into a regular low-cost payment. And you guys formulated a payment plan that was so low compared to what I was already paying anyway. It made it a no-brainer. So thank you, thank you, thank you for this. I highly suggest to everybody, call Shine Solar to get a quote. You would be amazed at the savings you will be able to generate!"

Nile H.

"Solar power is a big idea whose time has come . . . Imagine what it would be like if every time that it rained, it rained oil, big black drops falling from the sky. Don't you think that we would find some way to run around with a big bucket and collect all of that energy that was falling from the sky? I know this sounds like an absurd picture, but the reality is that what we have outside today is something very comparable to that. Literally, we have useful energy pouring out of the sky . . . . ."

GABRIELLE GIFFORDS, opening statement at meeting of Subcommittee on Energy and Environment, March 17, 2008

TABLE OF CONTENTS

Introduction

When I told my best friend that I was starting a solar company, he said, "Nick, please don't do it. We don't live in California or Arizona – this is Arkansas, and people here are not yet ready for solar power!"

As much as I love my friend and value his opinion and thoughts, I am so glad that I didn't listen to him. He was completely, totally, and irrefutably wrong. Here in Northwest Arkansas and Southwest Missouri, the demand for solar panel installation has been off the charts. Our company, Shine Solar, continues to hire installation crews and, at this writing, the demand shows no sign of slowing. As a solar business owner, this is thrilling!

But, after being involved in this for some time, I have found that there is a massive informational gap between the *perceived cost* of going solar and how much it *actually does cost*. This massive informational gap is keeping so many good people away from something that could benefit their family or business and lighten many a financial burden. Our mission at Shine Solar is to educate homeowners about how solar energy can save them money, increase the value of their home and make them more self-reliant. To help us fulfill this mission, I have written this book.

You've probably noticed the peculiar and predictable thing about technology — when it first comes out, it's expensive, it doesn't work very well, and it isn't easily available to the masses. The best example of that is Apple's iPhone. Back in 2007, when the iPhone came out, not only was it very expensive, but it couldn't do a fraction of what one can do today. The same applies to going solar. Over time, the cost has gone down, the efficiency has gone up, and it is available to the masses. Today, there are solar financing options available to people. Even just a year or two ago, these options weren't available.

So, all of these things are happening at the same time – all the necessary elements to make solar a reality for people are converging at once and are making going solar a realistic investment for people in Northwest Arkansas and Southwest Missouri. A very short time ago, these elements were non-existent. It is finally the time to go solar, not just because it is good for the environment and makes our carbon footprint smaller (although these are very worthy ideals), but because it is a sound financial practice and a good investment. Unfortunately, as is the case with many new ideas and concepts, there is a lack of understanding because of the lack of information. I hope this book answers some questions about solar energy and why it is not just affordable — it makes good financial sense.

For anyone who is looking to take greater control over his or her monthly utility bill and make a long-term, relatively low-risk investment, solar is the place you want to be. We are excited and honored to be a part of this movement. Read this book, and find out for yourself why you want to be involved in something that is changing the way Americans are consuming electricity. For more information, comments, and news, visit us on Facebook at facebook.com/Shinesolarpower/ or visit our website at www.shinesolar.com. Or just call us at 1-844-80-SHINE.

Nicholas Gorden

Shine Solar, LLC

CHAPTER 1

Let There Be Light

Since the beginning of time, people have used the sun's energy. Ancient people built their houses to face the sun. In the winter, their baked clay homes took in and stored the sun's heat. Today, the best-designed homes incorporate design elements to fully utilize the natural light of the sun. And, of course, lured by warm sunshine and green vistas, countless sun-seekers board planes, trains, and cruise ships to enjoy the warmer climates and escape from winter's chill.

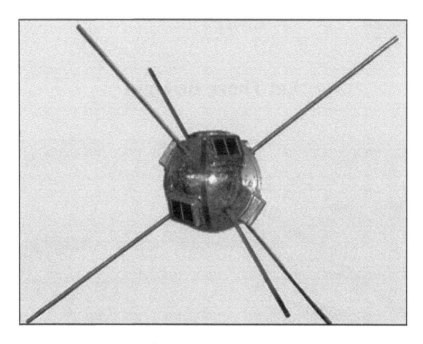

1958 Vanguard I Satellite
Credit: http://nssdc.gsfc.nasa.gov/nmc

Never doubting the power and importance of the sun, it did not take long for humans to experiment with solar power. In 1767, Horace de Saussure built the first solar oven by placing a number of black lined boxes, covered with glass, inside each other and then placed them in the sun. Inside the smallest box, the temperature rose above the boiling point of water! Others used this idea to create solar water heaters. In 1839, a man named Edmund Becquerel discovered the PHOTOVOLTAIC EFFECT when he discovered that certain materials produced electricity when put in sunlight. Scientists might have thought this was cool, but they really didn't know what to do with it — until the middle of the 20th century. In 1954, Bell Laboratories made the first solar cell out of silicon. Silicon is a pure form of sand. The silicon, the scientists discovered, was better than most materials at making electricity. Soon after this, when the U.S. space program needed a power source for satellites, guess what was used? Though solar cells were expensive, reliable power sources mattered more. In the 1950s, the space industry began to use solar technology to provide power aboard spacecraft. In 1958, the Vanguard 1 was launched, making it the first artificial earth satellite powered by solar cells. Today it is still up there and it remains the oldest manmade satellite in orbit — logging more than 6 billion miles.

CHAPTER 2

Early Adopters

Powering a space satellite with solar cells was exciting — it seemed an "electrifying" advancement. Surely, using solar energy to light our kitchens and heat our houses was not far behind! In the 1950's, after the launch of the Vanguard I, newspapers heralded the event and described fabulous scenarios where we would be soon harnessing the sun's limitless energy. People imagined we would soon power our sewing machines and watch new episodes of *Gunsmoke* using solar energy alone. In 1979, President Jimmy Carter installed 32 solar panels on the White House. At the time, he said, "A generation from now, this solar heater can either be a curiosity, a museum piece, an example of a road not taken, or it can be a small part of one of the greatest and most exciting adventures ever undertaken by the American people—harnessing the power of the sun to enrich our lives as we move away from our crippling dependence on foreign oil."

32 Panels Installed on the White House
by Jimmy Carter in 1979
Photo Credit: Jimmy Carter Presidential Library

If you are like us, you might be wondering which museum has those solar panels as an exhibit. Many innovators and experimenters continued to play with solar cells in the ensuing years. Unfortunately, solar panels remained expensive — out of the reach of many American people. Although they never actually went away, in the many decades following the launch of **Vanguard I** in the 1950s, the price of solar cells didn't exactly drop a great deal. The *idea* of solar energy was celebrated, touted, and idealized. The *practice* of it is was reserved for scientists with funding, the very wealthy, the very radical, and a few others with the wherewithal or knowledge about how to build and use them.

Those solar panels installed by Jimmy Carter were taken down during the second Reagan term and never reinstalled.

For a while, it seemed that the great promise of solar energy, touted by science and government, just would not materialize. Only in the past few years has "going solar" been, not only financially viable, but also financially prudent. It is no longer just an option for the rich and radical, but is now in the hands of ordinary, everyday working people like you and me. The American consumer has now arrived at the perfect crossroads of advanced and affordable solar technology, generous tax credits, and common sense financing. Going solar has gone mainstream. We at Shine Solar are proud to be at the forefront of this crossroads and pledge to steer you through the long-awaited and very exciting process of going solar. We invite you to visit our Facebook page at facebook.com/Shinesolarpower/ or visit our website at www.shinesolar.com. If you just want to talk to a human being, we get it! Call us at 1-844-80-SHINE.

PART II:
SOLAR ENERGY NOW

CHAPTER 3

Solar Power 101

Ask your kids, grandkids, or the neighborhood kids "What is solar energy?" And they will probably answer, correctly, "energy from the sun." They may even be able to describe (roughly) how a solar panel works (kids are so smart nowadays!). Practically everyone knows what it is. But before we delve into the details of solar panel installation, let's take a minute to lay some groundwork and really answer that question.

Solar energy is simply capturing the light from the sun — on a consistent and daily basis — and converting it into usable electricity that you can use to power your home every day. Solar cells, also called photovoltaic (PV) cells by scientists, convert sunlight directly into electricity. PV gets its name from the process of converting light (photons) to electricity (voltage), which is called the PV effect. The PV effect was discovered in 1954, when scientists at Bell Telephone discovered that silicon (an element found in sand) created an electric charge when exposed to sunlight. As we mentioned in the beginning of this book, soon solar cells were being used to power space satellites and smaller items like calculators and watches. For our purposes, and in the interests of remaining consistent, we will refer to all photovoltaic cells and the panels they are on, as "solar panels," which is what most Americans are familiar with.

Sunlight is considered direct current. That direct current energy shines down onto the solar panels and they, in turn, absorb that light. That current then gets channeled through to a device called an **inverter**. The job of an **inverter** is to switch **DC power to AC power**, which is the kind of power that we use in our homes. All of our outlets are AC power.

There are 3 basic parts to a solar energy system:

1. The **solar panels** that convert **light** into **power**;

2. The **racking** that the panels sit on, on a roof (the racking is actually connected to the shingles on the roof);

3. The wiring and cables that take that power to a device called an **inverter** whose job it is to flip the DC power we have taken from the sun into the AC power we use to power our home.

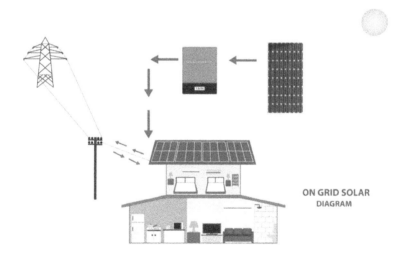

Credit: © Can Stock Photo / SirikulT

So, in the most simplified form, we take the power (or light) from the sun and we convert it into electricity that we can use every single day in our home.

Do you have more questions? Read on, or call us at 844-80-

SHINE and one of our professionals will be happy to explain solar panels in more detail. Visitors at Facebook.com/Shinesolarpower/ can find many, many videos explaining all the topics covered in this book (and then some!).

CHAPTER 4

Why Would I Want To Go Solar?

(Two words: Sense and Cents!)

Why Would People in Northwest Arkansas and Southwest Missouri Want to Go Solar? Why Would Anyone Want to Go Solar?

Historically, people went solar for at least three different reasons:

- They really wanted to get away from people. If you really want to get away from other people you have to go where there are no power lines, hence, no electricity. Hard-core hunters, fisherman and recreationists have long invested into off-grid solar systems to power their cabins and hidden getaways. Logic says that if you can afford to build a cabin in the woods then you can afford a solar system to power it. Although not economical, it's probably better than paying the utility company thousands of dollars to run power lines directly to your cabin.

- Some people just want to be prepared and there are few forms of self-reliance more dependable than generating your own electricity. Preppers like to be prepared for the worst and they want the peace-of-mind that comes with knowing that come hell or high water they will have electricity. Investing in solar for these people is nothing more than emergency preparedness.

- Everybody has a hobby, right? Hobbies, by definition, are fun to do but don't usually make you any money. Hobbyists turned to solar because they enjoyed playing with alternative forms of energy and liked the aspect of clean, renewable energy to power their homes, vehicles and toys. Often, someone "going solar" was dutifully outfitting his Berkeley, California, home to match or outdo his neighbor's expensive-but-very-eco-conscious home. Reducing a carbon footprint is a noble and worthy endeavor, but installing solar panels was often very costly — only those with an excess of cash could afford to do it. Not economical, but a ton of fun!

But times have changed and investing in a rooftop solar system has become an affordable, smart decision for most homeowners. The overall cost of solar panels and components has dropped by 70% since 2009, even as panels are getting more efficient.

Credit: fruttipics

As solar prices drop and utility prices increase across the country, the viability of going solar becomes a reality one market at a time. Solar has been a make-sense decision for a few years now in California, Arizona, New Jersey, Texas and several other states. Now Arkansas and Missouri are having their turn!

Our company, Shine Solar, is based in Northwest Arkansas — and we have recently opened a new office in Southwest Missouri. This is an area we serve and this is an area we have been raised in — an area we are raising our families in, too. The families that consume power in that area represent a fair cross-section of much of America. While they may all agree that reducing our dependence on fossil fuels is a worthy goal, common sense dictates that saving money for the children's education, planning for retirement, paying off a mortgage, and staying out of debt — not to mention putting food on the table, taking a vacation once in a while, and keeping a reliable car will take precedence over a carbon foot print reduction. The folks in the area make informed decisions — such as deciding to switch to solar energy or not — on important monetary outlays based on dollars and sense. So, if a project (such as installing solar panels) is going to cost them money, the return on their investment must be greater than the investment itself.

Another important reason to switch to solar is that you don't have to pay for your solar system upfront and in cash. Once again, times have changed. In the last couple of years solar loans have become prevalent in the market place. Now you can finance your entire solar system as long as you at least have a 660 credit score or higher, a respectable debt-to-income ratio, make at least 40k per year, and own your own home. No industry that sells high-ticket items has been able to flourish without attractive financing options (homes, cars, boats, appliances, home improvement, etc.). But, until recently there were no viable finance options for homeowners who wanted to purchase a solar system. Homeowners' only option was to write a check or take out a second mortgage against their home. None of these options sounds very attractive or fun. Solar loans have competitive interest rates, fees and most importantly, long-term paybacks that allow for energy savings to be realized the very first month after your system is installed. Some companies will even forgo payments for a full-year just so you can redeem your tax credits and start realizing some savings upfront. Competitive financing is the key to making a solar investment work for most families.

Credit: Pcanzo

In addition to common-sense financing, self-reliance, and cost-saving, consumers can save money in another way — by building equity. Occasionally, we'll have prospective customers tell us that it's not worth switching to solar unless they can save at least $100 per month (or $50, $75, $200, etc). But here's the deal, the amount of savings is irrelevant. In fact, as long as you're not paying MORE than what you pay the utility company you are coming out way ahead. We'll explain by asking you a question: Given the option, would you rather rent your home or own your home? Most of you, I'm guessing, would say "own" your home. Why? One simple word: EQUITY. When you own your home, even if you're making payments to the bank, every month you are getting a little closer to owning your home outright. Your monthly payments are eventually going to deliver you an asset free and clear. The person who rents will never own the home they live in no matter how many monthly payments they make to their landlord. It's no different with electricity. Would you rather "rent" your electricity every month from the utility company or eventually "own" your electricity, permanently? When you invest in a rooftop solar system you own the asset that will kick out electricity for thirty years or more!

And finally, in very recent years, thanks to reliable technology, generous government tax credits, and a practice in the utility company called "net metering," installing solar panels not only saves you money, but it also brings predictability to monthly energy payments. In the next chapters we will explain, in detail, exactly how this works to benefit you, the consumer. Although it has been a long time coming, the time for solar panels is finally upon us. We are writing this book to not only let people know about the bottom-line benefits they could receive from installing solar panels, but also to answer the many, many questions we have fielded from our customers and those who had doubts about the reliability or feasibility of solar panels. If, after reading this book, you want to know more, or if you want to hear from people like you who have installed solar panels, visit our Facebook page at facebook.com/Shinesolarpower/ or visit our website at www.shinesolar.com. Or, pick up the phone and call us at 844-80-SHINE.

Okay, Say I Take Out a Solar Loan ... Is There a Break-Even Point Once I Have Installed Solar Panels? When Is It?

There absolutely is. The only really honest way to look at it is this: *you are already paying the bill.* You make a payment every month to your utility company already, on a note that you will never pay off, with a payment that will always increase. There has never been an electricity *sale*. If you have solar power, in many cases your solar payment is *lower* than what you are paying for electric already. What's more, your solar bill will be paid off someday, and *free* for the rest of your life. So, the *immediate* break-even point is when your solar payment is the same as what you are paying to your utility landlord to rent your energy. From that point forth, you are better than the "break-even" point.

Well, What If I Don't Take Out a Loan? What If I Pay Cash for My Solar Panels? What is my Break-Even Point?

If you pay cash for a solar system that offsets 100% of your electricity usage, simply take the **total cost of your system (less the tax credit)** and **divide it by your last year's total annual electricity cost**. For example: If you invest $10,000 into a solar system, after your tax credit your total out-of-pocket cost will be $7,000 (applying the 30% federal tax credit). Now, divide that $7,000 by last year's annual electricity bill (Let's say that it was $2,000). The answer is 3.5 — it would take you 3.5 years to break-even on your investment.

$10,000 (solar system cost) – $3,000 (30% tax credit) = $7,000 (total-out-of-pocket cost)

$7,000 (total-out-of-pocket cost) ÷ 2,000 (previous year's cost of electricity) = 3.5 years

Answer: 3.5 years until break-even is realized

Keep in mind, however, that these numbers are estimates and for illustration purposes only. You will achieve an even faster break-even if the utility company raises their rates in between the date you installed your system and your original estimated break-even point.

In both scenarios, whether you finance your solar system with a solar loan or buy it outright, the break-even point will be influenced by a variety of factors, such as how much electricity is used in a given year, the cost of your solar system, how much electricity is used and offset, the price the utility company is charging for electricity, etc. When you have more information about your system and your electricity needs, you can more accurately measure the break-even point. If you live in one of the areas that Shine Solar services, take advantage of our offer to get a free quote on how solar panels can help get you to that "promised land" first described so many decades ago by hopeful scientists, researchers, and environmentalists. To speak with a person, call 1-844-80-SHINE or book your discovery call online at www.shinesolar.com.

CHAPTER 5

Is Going Solar Right For Me?

(Mostly yes, but a no is not unheard of)

We wrote this book, in part, to better answer the many questions we get from people who are thinking about making the investment into installing solar panels on their home. Understandably, people are more than a little hesitant and they have questions about the financial feasibility of switching. People have many "what if?" scenarios. Folks have many questions about us, too. They wanted to know about warranties and if they are available (of course, and if you are in another part of the country, and you are reading this, please make sure your installer offers a good one), the length of a typical warranty. They wanted to know what kind of things could go wrong, and what kind of things could go right.

When consumers begin to consider: "Is going solar is right for me?" the top three questions they ask are:

1. How reliable is it? How long does it last?

2. Does my house qualify?

3. How much does it cost?

1. How reliable is it?

At Shine Solar, we use a Tier 1 photovoltaic panel. This panel has a 25-year linear performance warrantee. Generally, in order for a Tier 1 panel to be designated as such, the manufacturer of the product meets the following criteria:

- Has been producing solar panels for 5 years or more;

- Are either publically listed on a stock exchange or have a strong and stable balance sheet;

- Has fully automated production and a high degree of vertical integration;

- Has invested significantly in brand marketing

Tier 2 or Tier 3 manufacturers are those who do not meet one or more of these criteria.

When using a Tier 1 panel with a 25-year warranty, it means that every year, for the next 25 years, they are guaranteed to produce a certain amount of power. So, in year 16, if they are not producing what they are supposed to, we will come out, fix it, repair it, and/or replace it, at no cost to you. They are also virtually maintenance free, because there are no moving parts. They are built out of a poly and a mono crystalline silicone — they are built to last. They are engineered to go on rooftops and solar farms for decades. They are covered with tempered glass and were built to take a beating. But 25 years is a long time, so how is the solar production quantity monitored? How do you know what they are producing? The answer is that a monitor is actually built inside your system — we can track and monitor solar production. In addition, we give you the ability to track and monitor the production using an iPhone or android app. You can log in and see how much is being produced. Our customers do it all the time and report back to us. And can you imagine the thrill and satisfaction they feel when they see their meter going **backwards**?

Credit: nbehmans

Even with a warranty, many would-be customers think, "What about extreme weather? How reliable are the panels in a hailstorm?" In response, we like to make the comparison to a car driving through a hailstorm. If you are driving through a hailstorm, your car will most certainly get dented and pinged, but most of our windshields are not getting shattered. Why? Because the tempered glass is made to withstand the elements, it is *made* to be outside — a solar panel is worthless indoors. Of course, when you go solar, you will notify your homeowner's insurance. When our family put panels up, the homeowner's insurance went up about 3 dollars a month. So, if I am calling in hailstorm claims for my roof, homeowner's insurance is going to cover it. Furthermore, the racking system we use at Shine Solar is rated over 100 miles per hour. If any of those weather elements are happening in your area and around your home, you will most certainly have more serious worries than the reliability of your solar panels. In our area of Northwest Arkansas and Southwest Missouri, in over one year of installing solar panels, we have never had a customer who experienced a weather-related incident and had to replace a panel or call us to report a manufacturer's defect.

2. Does my house (or my roof) qualify?

Another frequently asked question is: "Does my house qualify?" When considering an install, we look at how much roof space you have and what the shading situation is around your roof. If you have a lot of trees surrounding your house or if the existing trees make a canopy over your roof, it is most likely not an excellent roof for solar because the shading will impact how much solar energy is put out. Our software takes guessing out of the equation, and we can give you an accurate estimate before we even come out to your house. As with any reputable company, many of our tools have been put in place to really nail down a number and tell you how much solar energy you can expect your rooftop panels to produce. Whether you have enough roof to put panels on to offset 10 percent of your power or 100 percent of your power, we will let you know. Keep in mind, however, even if it is only 10 percent, that is 10 percent of the power that you will own the source of and you won't have to purchase that percentage of power from the utility company – when there is a rate hike (and there always is), you won't be subject to the rate hike for that 10%, 50%, 75%, or 100%.

On occasion, we do tell people that their roofs are just not a good option for solar panels. Sometimes houses are just not a good fit for solar panels – if you have a house where the amount of sun exposure, roof surface area, or climate inhibits the amount of solar energy that solar panels will generate, we will tell you. We must — our warranty is tied to it.

Of course, if your roof *is* a good candidate for solar panels, we will not only tell you, we will you let you know how much solar power the panels on your roof will generate. So, if you use a typical amount of power each month, and you don't have a lot of trees surrounding your house, it usually makes complete sense to go solar.

3. How much does it cost?

The two most common questions asked about installing solar panels are, "How much does it cost?" and "Can I afford it?" Before estimating the cost of a system, we always like to make sure consumers understand that a federal tax credit is available for homeowners who install solar energy systems. The credit is for 30% through 2019, then decreases to 26% for tax year 2020, then to 22% for tax year 2021. It expires December 31, 2021. What this means is that if your system will cost $20,000, then $6,000 dollars will go back to you, the solar panel purchaser, instead of going back to the IRS — if they are installed before tax year 2020. If they are installed in tax year 2021, you will have earned a tax credit of $4,400. Learn more at https://energy.gov/savings/residential-renewable-energy-tax-credit. In addition, there are numerous state and local incentives. Depending on where you live and what programs are offered, you could find yourself with even more money saving incentives. You can find state and local incentives at https://energy.gov/savings/search. Of course, our sales team also knows the incentives in the area they serve and can cite them, chapter and verse. It makes us very happy to see our hardworking neighbors benefit from all incentives and tax credits offered — for far too long, electricity consumers in our area got a bad deal — we believe it's time to make better deals!

Credit: malerapaso/E+/getty images

If it sounds like it's too good to be true, we understand. It's a new concept! If you are used to getting power in one way from one source because that is the way it has happened your whole life, it *is* hard to get used to. The concept is new, the technology has improved, the current tax credits can't be beat, and a company like Shine Solar is telling you that you can spend the same or less each month and **buy** a solar system for your house that you will eventually **own**? But yes, that is it.

We once heard someone call the concept of solar energy a scam. We thought, "Yeah, we bet someone would think that because it sounds way too good to be true."

As far as the question of what the actual cost of the system is, before rebates and incentives, the *easiest* answer is that the cost will vary depending on the size of your solar system; the bigger the system, the greater the cost. System costs range from a few thousand dollars up to tens of thousands of dollars. The cost of a solar energy system depends on your electricity needs and your goal (reduce electricity bills or completely eradicate them?). And, of course, each rooftop is different, so we'll design and engineer a tailor-made system to fit your roof. The best news is that we provide easy and affordable solar loan financing if you don't have upfront cash to pay for your system.

To many, installing rooftop solar panels seems like a big project that costs a lot of money. Recognizing that this was a deterrent for many customers, Shine Solar developed a "no money out-of-pocket, 100% financing" option. With this program and our solar loan, we can finance the entire project. This means that you can get solar panels installed, monitored, and warranteed without a dime ever leaving your pocket. We replace a goodly portion of your payment to the utility company with a fixed solar panel payment — and that number is *never* going to go up. So, how does this compare to making a payment to the utility company? The loan payment that you make on your solar panels will not fluctuate, unlike the utility company who can impose a rate hike that is reflected in your electric bill. Remember, they own the electricity, so they can charge you more for it. They don't have to ask for your permission, either. In our area of Northwest Arkansas, utility costs go up, on average, about 4 to 4.5% a year. It is not much, but the increase is always there and it has continued to rise for the past few decades. The utility company is a monopoly. You must pay the bill and their percentage increase or they shut off your power. If that happens, your food goes bad, and your lights go out, and your air conditioner doesn't work.

Faced with these realities, we have asked ourselves, "Am

I ever not going to **not** need power?" The answer is no, of course, so if we replace a good chunk of our power bill with a fixed solar panel payment then we can lock in our price for power — and it will be the same 5 years from now or 10 years from now. The best part is this: Once the solar loan is paid off, there won't even be a power bill anymore. This is how we can pay off our power bill with solar — we own our own power AND the installed solar panel system adds instant equity to our home. A consumer takes on debt for a short time by taking out a loan. Eventually, it is paid off, and now he is not renting the power from the power plant, he actually *owns* his own power — he has his own power plant! So you are not buying power from Shine Solar, you are buying a power plant that generates your power. As believers in the freedom and self-reliance that a solar loan can give to a person, we want to emphasize that this it is not another outflow of cash — you are already paying money, on a monthly basis, to your power company.

Understandably, some people feel uncomfortable with the idea of a loan. Many say that they don't want or need another loan. We get that! Many among us cringe at the idea of debt — and when we hear the word "finance," we run. Like you, we do not want to be in debt or to owe anyone any money. Consider this, however: your utility bill is not considered a "debt" even though you will pay one for the rest of your life in your home, no matter what. If you are reading this, you probably have an electric bill. What this is designed to do is offset the electric bill with the solar payment instead. Now, every month when you make the solar payment you are buying something — you are building equity in something, you will ultimately own it. It is very nearly the same concept as going to get a mortgage vs. renting a house. For instance, one of our partners has a 30-year mortgage on his house. He is certain that he does not plan to stay in that house for thirty years, but it still made sense for him to get a mortgage and buy the house. Why?

Because when he does go to sell his house in 5, 10, or 15 years, he will get back out of it whatever he put into it. This same concept operates in a solar loan. The loan is paid off in loan payments. The money earmarked for the loan payment each month replaces the money that you are *already paying to the power company*. You are already handing money over to them! In essence, your utility payment is a 100% interest-only payment to the power company. How? Because at the end of 15, 20, or 30 years, the utility company will not hand over a deed to the company and congratulate you on full ownership. In contrast, when your solar loan is paid off, you will own your own source of power. Those monocrystalline and polycrystalline solar panels on your roof are *yours*, as well as the electricity they generate.

When a solar company sits down with you, as we do, they will break down how much you pay, how much you will save, how much the solar panels will cost and what your utility bills will look like post-installation. A good company can tell you how much you will save, not only over the next month, but over the next 5, 10, or 20 years. Like us, that solar company should be in it with you for the long haul. An excellent company will go above and beyond "good." For instance, at Shine Solar, we take care of our customers before, during, and after the install. We offer a workmanship warranty for **12 years** after the install. A warranty this long means a company will stand behind their work and the products that they use. Finally, if you get solar panels installed by Shine Solar and then, within five years of the install, decide that you need to get your roof replaced, we will do all of the **reinstall work free of charge within five years of the solar panel installation**. We are not kidding. To read more about our guaranties, visit our website at shinesolar.com/guaranties.

Credit: istockphoto/cacaroot

We know this is virtually unheard of, and we stand behind our work and the products we use, but we also believe in superb customer care. Part of that care is offering to reinstall those solar panels within five years if you decide your roof needs replacing. This is a rarity in the solar panel installation business, but, as our company motto says, "We install happiness." So we will go right ahead and *reinstall* happiness, too. If you live in another part of the country that is not serviced by Shine Solar, LLC, please be sure to ask about warranties and peace-of-mind guarantees. If you want to read more about the "happiness" we install, you can find the comments of our happy solar-powered customers on our Facebook page at facebook.com/Shinesolarpower/

CHAPTER 6

The Nuts and Bolts of Solar Panels

How it works

Photo credit: Elenathewise

How Do Solar Panels Work? / What is a Photovoltaic (PV) System?

As a homeowner or business owner who is considering the installation of solar panels, you are probably wondering how solar works. After all, before you make such a hefty investment in harnessing the sun's power, you want to be sure you have a solid understanding of how solar works and how it can serve as a cost-effective option for you and your home or business.

Exploring the Basics of How Solar Works

Solar energy is created when sunlight hits an electron in the first layer of a solar panel, which is made up of many small solar cells that are made of two different layers stuck together. When the sunlight hits the electron, it causes the electron to jump to the second layer. This electron then makes another electron move, which causes another to move. This chain reaction ultimately results in a flow of electrons, which translates to electricity. This electricity is then used to power your home or business.

Powering Your Home with Solar Energy

What are the components of a roof top solar system (PV system)?

The basic building block of solar panels (or photovoltaic (PV) modules) is the "solar cell" — also called the "PV cell." The two terms, "PV" and "solar," are often used interchangeably, but for the purposes of this book, we will use "solar," since that is what most people are familiar with. Multiple solar cells are connected to form a solar panel (or PV module), which is the smallest solar component sold commercially. Modules range in power output from about 250 watts to 325 watts. After the electricity is produced by your solar panels, the current leaves the solar panel and passes through a wire conduit. This wire leads to an inverter, which is capable of inverting the direct current (DC) with a fixed voltage into an alternating current (AC). The current then feeds into your home's circuitry or into an electrical grid, which can then be used to power your appliances and everything else in your home in the same way as the electricity that you receive from your local utility company.

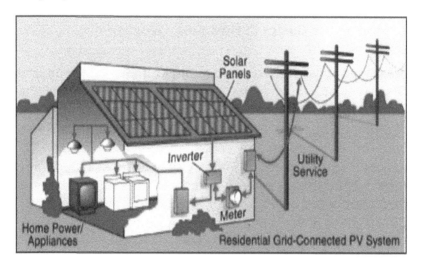

Courtesy: U.S. Department of Energy

Okay, I have a pretty good idea of how solar panels work, but what about . . .?

At this point in the process, many folks have a good understanding of how solar works and how they can get it to work for them. More detailed questions pop up, however, and many people can't find the answers on a .gov website or in a brochure. At Shine Solar, our company motto is "Installing happiness." We believe an informed solar customer is a happy solar customer, so we will share some customers' questions and concerns here. As always, if you are reading this book and you have questions that aren't answered here, please email, message, or call. We are found on Facebook at facebook.com/Shinesolarpower/ or you can visit our website at www.shinesolar.com. If you want to talk to a real, live person call 1-844-80-SHINE. We can't wait to hear from you!

Where are the solar panels made?

Much like all appliances in your home, modules are globally sourced. We have access to panels made from many different countries, including the United States. Research tells us, however, that the country of origin has no correlation with quality.

- **What are they made of?**

  Panels are made from three layers of silicon and glass that is 15 times more tempered than the windshield on your car. Solar panels are engineered to be outside *and* working for 30 years or more! (These guys are tough.)

- **Will there be an *"iPhone effect"* with these panels? New and better gadgets come out every year — if I install now, will I be stuck with old, slow, clunky panels?**

  The reason we have to upgrade our iPhones (or androids) and computers is because we want them to do something more than when we originally bought them. The first iPhone couldn't even take video — but this didn't stop demand. Today, most people wouldn't even *consider* buying a Smartphone without video capabilities.

  Solar panels are different. With solar panels, we will always want them to do *exactly* the same thing as the very first day we installed them, which is to create and provide energy. We can't imagine we'd want them to take video of our kids' soccer games! The earliest solar panels are still producing, decades

later. This is just one more benefit of solar panels —
they need no upgrade.

- **Will my roof support this? What kind of roof do I
need?**

Some types of roofs are
simpler and cheaper to work
with, but solar panels can be
installed on any type. The
experienced installers at
Shine Solar, LLC know how
to work on all types and can
use roofing techniques that eliminate any possibility
of leaks.

- **How do you know that the solar panels are not
too heavy to be supported by my roof?**

Solar panels weigh in at less than another layer of
shingles, at about three pounds per square foot. They
are extremely light . . . less than a fat cat walking on
your roof.

- **How will installing the solar panels affect the roof
warranty?**

You will need to consult your roofing company
and/or manufacturer, but in almost every case, it will
not affect the warranty. The flashings and fasteners
that Shine Solar uses are the industry standard for
affixing the array to your roof so that it lasts a
lifetime.

- **What if my roof is older?**

Typically, if your roof is older and needs to be replaced in the near future, a solar installation company will tell you that you should replace it at the time your solar panels are installed to avoid the cost of removing and reinstalling your solar panels. Of course, if your roof needs to be replaced, by all means do it! But every solar company is different when it comes to how much they charge to uninstall, store, and reinstall your solar panels should you need a new roof. Be sure to ask for those details up front if you think you may need a new roof! The last thing you want is to have to replace a roof a few years after an install and then get hit with hefty reinstallation fees! At Shine Solar, we know this can be a worry and a concern to our customers. One of the many qualities that separate Shine Solar from other solar installation companies is that we offer a 5-year roof replacement guarantee, which states that ***should any customer of ours need a new roof within the first 5-years of their original installation date Shine Solar will remove, store and reinstall the solar panels free of charge***. Want to read more about our stellar guaranties? Visit our web page at shinesolar.com/guaranties.

CHAPTER 7

Your Home and The Grid

Do I need special insurance? Will my homeowner's insurance go up?

You will most certainly need to inform your homeowner's insurance company when you install a solar system on your roof. The increase in monthly cost is minimal, but it is impossible to pinpoint what each individual will pay. As you research and do due diligence, a call to your homeowner's company is certainly in order.

Will my home be worth more or less?

It is impossible to predict what your home will be worth or what your home will sell for. However, we have noted that in other areas, if a home has a rooftop solar system already installed *and* it is included in the purchase price of the house, the home will generally sell for more than comparable houses in the neighborhood. The evidence suggests that homebuyers like the idea of purchasing a house with solar panels, but this affinity for the panels goes away quickly if the photovoltaic panels are leased.

Credit: fruttipics

Going Off or Staying On the Grid

Most homeowners choose to stay "on the grid" after installing a solar panel system. As we mentioned, many of those who want to remove themselves completely from society fall into groups like "preppers," survivalists, extreme sportsman, and some radical fringe groups. There are exceptions, of course! Some people, no matter the cost, just do not want any contact with a utility company. Hey, we get it and we can help you achieve that, but the vast majority of people who come to Shine Solar with an interest in solar power are looking to reduce or eliminate their bill from the utility company. The satisfaction of self-sufficiency and independence from the bills and rate hikes of their utility company is the goal they are after. Therefore, the great majority will choose to stay "on the grid."

Photo credit: http://www.energy.gov

When you stay on the grid, your home continues to be powered by the electric company. When your home makes solar energy, that energy is fed back to the grid and credited toward your account. In this way, you are guaranteed to have a constant flow of energy — even on days that are exceptionally cloudy and during the nighttime. You pay for what you use — on some days you use nothing and even produce more than you need. This is also credited back to your account If you choose to go "off the grid," you will need to have batteries that are capable of storing power to be used during those times when your solar module cannot capture enough energy from the sun to fulfill your needs at the time.

How Do You Estimate How Much Energy a Panel Will Produce?

On average, modern photovoltaic (PV) solar panels will produce 8 - 10 watts per square foot of solar panel area. For example, a roof area of 20 feet by 10 feet is 200 square-feet (20 ft x 10 ft). This would produce, roughly, 9 watts per sq-foot, or 200 sq-ft x 9 watts/sq-ft = 1,800 watts (1.8 kW) of electric power.

Converting Power (watts or kW) to Energy (kWh)

One kilowatt-hour (1 kWh) means an energy source supplies 1,000 watts (1 kW) of energy for one hour. Generally, a solar energy system will provide output for about 5 hours per day. So, if you have a 1.8 kW system size and it produces for 5 hours a day, 365 days a year: This solar energy system will produce 3,285 kWh in a year (1.8 kW x 5 hours x 365 days).

If the solar panels are shaded for part of the day, the output would be reduced in accordance to the shading percentage. For example, if the solar panels receive 4 hours of direct sunshine a day (versus the standard 5 hours), the panels are shaded 1 divided by 5 = 20% of the time (80% of assumed direct sun shine hours received). In this case, the output of a 200 square-foot PV panel system would be 3,285 kWh per year x 80% = 2,628 kWh per year.

What happens to my solar if my power goes out?

Typically, if your power is out, your solar is out. Why? When the power goes out, grid-tied solar systems also shut off — but not because they can't produce electricity. The systems are programmed to turn off automatically for safety reasons. When the power goes out, electricity for those sections of the grid are shut off so that workers can try to fix the issue. If solar systems stay on, and continue to send electricity through the wires while they are being repaired, you run the risk of electrocuting the workers. Fortunately, power does not go off all that often, so there is no need to worry about this scenario any more than you did when you were getting your electricity from the grid.

The only time the power would stay on is if you have a backup generator or a battery backup system. While this choice is entirely yours, we have found both options to be expensive — negating the savings you would enjoy from generating your own electricity. Of course, if your goal is to be completely self-reliant and off the power grid, speak to the professionals at Shine Solar, LLC and inform them of your needs — they will be glad to assist! Visit our Facebook page at facebook.com/Shinesolarpower/ or visit our website at www.shinesolar.com. Or, just pick up your phone and call us at 1-844-80-SHINE.

CHAPTER 8

Net Metering Explained

Photo credit: ©can stock photo/ epantha

The world runs off of technology, and because of that we depend on electricity to power everything we use. Solar energy plays an important and growing role in our nation's energy, but without the help and cooperation from local utilities, homeowners like you and me couldn't save money just by switching to solar.

In this section, we will cover a term that is widely used in the solar industry. However, to industry outsiders, it is a term that is not widely recognized. The term we are talking about is "**net metering**." Let's break it down into three simple parts: What it is, why it's awesome, and how it works.

Every morning, when sunlight hits the solar panels, the panels convert the sun's energy into electricity that can be used to power your home. During the day, if the solar system's production exceeds the house's power needs, the excess power is fed back into the grid. When this occurs, you can observe the electrical meter spin backwards. In other words, you are viewing **net metering in action**. Most local governments have a system of credits set in place that require utility companies to buy this excess energy back. In addition to reducing your electric bill, these credits can be sold to utilities. This generates revenue to pay back your investment for the solar system and, eventually, turn a profit.

At night, or anytime a house is using more electricity than a solar system is producing, if the house is using more electricity than the solar system is producing, the excess energy needed to power the house is pulled from the grid, as it normally would be. When you install a solar system on a home, the only noticeable difference you'll see is on your electricity bill. Investing in a photovoltaic solar system is a smart choice that pays for itself over time by harnessing the most abundant free form of energy available to us today — solar power.

There are some times when solar panels generate more power than you need at home. This energy is put to good use. **Net metering** makes sure you receive the credit on your power bills for the energy you put back on the grid. It's like rollover minutes for solar. This credit fairly compensates all kinds of energy users from a small homes and big businesses to schools and public buildings. The credits you accumulate in a given month can offset the charges you receive in future months. These credits are all tracked via the net meter installed by the local utility. To ensure these credits are measured accurately, clients have the ability to track all production from the system, via the web monitoring, for accuracy. But whatever kind of solar household or business you are, there is one more thing to know. Everyone with solar can save money on energy while making a difference in the environment.

Read comments about (and experiences with) net metering from Shine Solar customers on our Facebook page at facebook.com/Shinesolarpower/. Of course, if the telephone is your preference, call us at 1-844-80-SHINE.

CHAPTER 9

I See The Light (and the savings)!

What to expect when you decide to install solar panels

I See the Light! I Am Going to Install Solar Panels! What's Next?

If you have read through this entire book, or just enough to realize that installing solar panels is the solution to your erratic and too-high electricity bills, then call Shine Solar at 1-844-80-SHINE. They will review your bills and inspect your property (including the roof) and offer you a proposal that will spell out all the details and definitely answer the question whether or not going solar is a smart move for you. You can also book a discovery call online at http://www.shinesolar.com. When Shine Solar is your installation company, here are the five brief stages that will take place:

1. **Survey.** Shine Solar wants to make sure what we have proposed will work. Our company will take some measurements, check out your roof, and do a

shade analysis.

2. **Permitting**. Depending on where you live, in most cases the solar installation company will need to pull a permit since they will be doing electrical work. At Shine Solar, we handle all of this on our end with our Master Electricians.

3. **Installation**. In most circumstances, this is a 1 to 2 day process. We will install the panels and tie it in to the electrical system of the home.

4. **Inspection**. Under the circumstances where a permit is required, we will request a city or county inspection to ensure we have done everything to code. This typically occurs within 24-48 hours of the completed installation.

5. **Interconnection**. This is the big day! A representative from the utility company will come to do their inspection, swap out your meter and turn it all on. Your system is LIVE!

Our process and the way our team handles solar panel installation has been lauded and celebrated by many of our neighbors and friends. We love to share the praises we've gotten from satisfied homeowners all over Northwest Arkansas and Southwest Missouri. We like to hear how well we've done, but we also know that the praise and satisfaction from others helps our customers feel more confident to make the decision to go solar. Of course, a reduced or negative utility bill will do more wonders for love of solar power than positive reviews, but the satisfaction and success of regular, everyday working people is often an important starting point. At the end of this chapter, we have included some comments customers have written about Shine Solar.

We hope that this book has answered your questions and has given you easy-to-understand information about installing solar panels — we believe in our product and our people, and we hope you will, too. For more reviews, comments, and just plain happiness visit Shine Solar, LLC on our Facebook page at https://www.facebook.com/Shinesolarpower/. We'd love to hear your comments and, if we can answer your questions, we will.

What People Are Saying About Solar Panels and Shine Solar, LLC?

"This has been a great company to work with. They do all the work and we get all the credit! One day installation — no money up front — home value increased — lowered energy cost and a 30% tax credit. Why wouldn't you go solar?"

Lori J.

"We have had such a great experience with the team from Shine Solar — from sales to installation. The sales representative helped us with working out the best number of panels to meet the goals we were looking for. The actual installation was complete in one day by very a professional and polite team.

They even had a service rep, Faith, meet the electric company at our home the day of start up. We love the ability to see our power usage, or should I say savings, on line, at my convenience."

Mary P.C.

"I'm so excited that Shine Solar is here in NWA (Northwest Arkansas) and helping bring awareness that Solar power is an affordable option to help lower your energy bill right here in our area! If you have the need, contact them! So excited that they have made it all so easy!"

Sage B.O.

"I went solar with Shine this summer and it has been a great experience! Their original proposal for how much money I would save has been spot on. My billing cycle with the local utility was a little funny for the first 2 months after installation (a 10 day cycle, then a 50 day cycle), but on my first normal cycle my electric utility bill was only $13. My utility payment plus my solar loan payment is less than I was paying for electricity before. Better yet, when my solar loan is paid off I'll ONLY be paying roughly $13 per month for my electricity! Shine Solar was great to work with and everything they told me would happen has happened just as they said it would."

Jared G.

SOLAR GLOSSARY*

The solar glossary contains definitions for technical terms related to solar power and photovoltaic (PV) technologies, including terms having to do with electricity, power generation, and concentrating solar power (CSP). It is reprinted from **https://energy.gov/eere/sunshot/solar-energy-glossary** and is not included in the_copyrighted material of this book.

III-V cell — A high-efficiency solar cell made from materials including Group III and Group V elements from the periodic table.

A

absorber — In a **photovoltaic device**, the material that readily absorbs **photons** to generate charge carriers (free **electrons** or **holes**).

AC — *See* **alternating current**.

acceptor — A dopant material, such as boron, which has fewer outer shell electrons than required in an otherwise balanced crystal structure, providing a hole, which can accept a free electron.

activated shelf life — The period of time, at a specified temperature, that a charged battery can be stored before its capacity falls to an unusable level.

activation voltage(s) — The **voltage(s)** at which a **charge controller** will take action to protect the batteries.

adjustable set point — A feature allowing the user to

adjust the **voltage** levels at which a **charge controller** will become active.

acceptor — A **dopant** material, such as **boron**, which has fewer outer shell **electrons** than required in an otherwise balanced crystal structure, providing a **hole**, which can accept a free **electron**.

AIC — *See* **amperage interrupt capability**.

air mass (sometimes called air mass ratio) — Equal to the cosine of the **zenith angle**-that angle from directly overhead to a line intersecting the sun. The air mass is an indication of the length of the path solar radiation travels through the atmosphere. An air mass of 1.0 means the sun is directly overhead and the radiation travels through one atmosphere (thickness).

alternating current (AC) — A type of **electrical current**, the direction of which is reversed at regular intervals or cycles. In the United States, the standard is 120 reversals or 60 cycles per second. Electricity transmission networks use AC because **voltage** can be controlled with relative ease.

ambient temperature — The temperature of the surrounding area.

amorphous semiconductor — A non-crystalline **semiconductor** material that has no long-range order.

amorphous silicon — A **thin-film**, **silicon photovoltaic cell** having no crystalline structure. Manufactured by depositing layers of **doped silicon** on a **substrate**. *See also* **single-crystal silicon** an **polycrystalline silicon**.

amperage interrupt capability (AIC) — **direct current** fuses should be rated with a sufficient AIC to interrupt the highest possible current.

ampere (amp) — A unit of **electrical current** or rate of flow of **electrons**. One **volt** across one **ohm** of resistance causes a current flow of one ampere.

ampere-hour (Ah/AH) — A measure of the flow of current (in **amperes**) over one hour; used to measure **battery** capacity.

ampere hour meter — An instrument that monitors current with time. The indication is the product of current (in **amperes**) and time (in hours).

ancillary services — Services that assist the **grid** operator in maintaining system balance. These include regulation and the contingency reserves: spinning, non-spinning, and in some regions, supplemental operating reserve.

angle of incidence — The angle that a ray of sun makes with a line perpendicular to the surface. For example, a surface that directly faces the sun has a solar angle of incidence of zero, but if the surface is parallel to the sun (for example, sunrise striking a horizontal rooftop), the angle of incidence is 90°.

annual solar savings — The annual solar savings of a solar building is the energy savings attributable to a solar feature relative to the energy requirements of a non-solar building.

anode — The positive **electrode** in an **electrochemical cell** (battery). Also, the earth or ground in a **cathodic protection** system. Also, the positive terminal of a **diode**.

antireflection coating — A thin coating of a material applied to a **solar cell** surface that reduces the light reflection and increases light transmission.

array — *See* **photovoltaic (PV) array**.

array current — The **electrical current** produced by a **photovoltaic array** when it is exposed to sunlight.

array operating voltage — The **voltage** produced by a **photovoltaic array** when exposed to sunlight and connected to a **load**.

autonomous system — *See* **stand-alone system**.

availability — The quality or condition of a **photovoltaic system** being available to provide power to a **load**. Usually measured in hours per year. One minus availability equals downtime.

azimuth angle — The angle between true south and the point on the horizon directly below the sun.

B

balance of system — Represents all components and costs other than the **photovoltaic modules/array**. It includes design costs, land, site preparation, system installation, support structures, power conditioning, operation and maintenance costs, indirect storage, and related costs.

balancing area — A metered segment of the power system, maintained by a balancing area authority, that ensures the total of all electrical generation equals the total of all system loads.

band gap — In a **semiconductor**, the energy difference between the highest band and the lowest **conduction band**.

band gap energy (Eg) — The amount of energy

(in **electron volts**) required to free an outer shell **electron** from its orbit about the nucleus to a free state, and thus promote it from the **valence** to the **conduction level**.

barrier energy — The energy given up by an **electron** in penetrating the **cell barrier**; a measure of the electrostatic potential of the barrier.

base load — The average amount of electric power that a utility must supply in any period.

base load generating plants — Typically coal or nuclear generating units that are committed and dispatched at constant or near-constant levels with minimum cycling. They are often the sources of lowest-cost of energy when run at very high **capacity factors**.

battery — Two or more **electrochemical cells** enclosed in a container and electrically interconnected in an appropriate series/parallel arrangement to provide the required operating **voltage** and current levels. Under common usage, the term battery also applies to a single cell if it constitutes the entire electrochemical storage system.

battery available capacity — The total maximum charge, expressed in **ampere-hours**, that can be withdrawn from a cell or **battery** under a specific set of operating conditions including **discharge rate**, temperature, initial **state of charge**, age, and cut-off **voltage**.

battery capacity — The maximum total electrical charge, expressed in **ampere-hours**, which a **battery** can deliver to a **load** under a specific set of conditions.

battery cell — The simplest operating unit in a storage **battery**. It consists of one or more positive **electrodes** or plates, an **electrolyte** that permits ionic conduction, one or more negative electrodes or plates, separators between plates of opposite polarity, and a container for all the above.

battery cycle life — The number of cycles, to a specified **depth of discharge**, that a cell or **battery** can undergo before failing to meet its specified capacity or efficiency performance criteria.

battery energy capacity — The total energy available, expressed in **watt-hours** (**kilowatt-hours**), which can be withdrawn from a fully charged cell or **battery**. The energy capacity of a given **cell** varies with temperature, rate, age, and cut-off **voltage**. This term is more common to system designers than it is to the **battery** industry where capacity usually refers to **ampere-hours**.

battery energy storage — Energy storage using electrochemical **batteries**. The three main applications for battery energy storage systems include spinning reserve at generating stations, **load** leveling at substations, and peak shaving on the customer side of the meter.

battery life — The period during which a **cell** or **battery** is capable of operating above a specified capacity or efficiency performance level. Life may be measured in cycles and/or years, depending on the type of service for which the cell or battery is intended.

BIPV — *See* **building integrated photovoltaics**.

blocking diode — A **semiconductor** connected in series with a **solar cell** or cells and a storage **battery** to keep the **battery** from discharging through the **cell** when there is no output, or low output, from the **solar cell**. It can be thought of as a one-way valve that allows **electrons** to flow forwards, but not backwards.

boron (B) — The chemical element commonly used as the **dopant** in **photovoltaic device** or **cell** material.

boule — A sausage-shaped, synthetic single-crystal mass grown in a special furnace, pulled and turned at a rate necessary to maintain the single-crystal structure during growth.

British thermal unit (Btu) — The amount of heat required to raise the temperature of one pound of water one degree Fahrenheit; equal to 252 calories.

building integrated photovoltaics — A term for the design and integration of **photovoltaic**(PV) technology into the building envelope, typically replacing conventional building materials. This integration may be in vertical facades, replacing view glass, spandrel glass, or other facade material; into semitransparent skylight systems; into roofing systems, replacing traditional roofing materials; into shading "eyebrows" over windows; or other building envelope systems.

bypass diode — A **diode** connected across one or more **solar cells** in a photovoltaic module such that the diode will conduct if the **cell**(s) become reverse biased. It protects these solar cells from thermal destruction in case of total or partial shading of individual solar cells while other cells are exposed to full light.

C

cadmium (Cd) — A chemical element used in making certain types of **solar cells** and batteries.

cadmium telluride (CdTe) — A polycrystalline thin-film photovoltaic material.

capacity (C) — *See* <u>battery capacity</u>.

capacity factor — The ratio of the average load on (or power output of) an electricity generating unit or system to the capacity rating of the unit or system over a specified period of time.

captive electrolyte battery — A battery having an immobilized <u>electrolyte</u> (gelled or absorbed in a material).

cathode — The negative pole or <u>electrode</u> of an electrolytic <u>cell</u>, vacuum tube, etc., where <u>electrons</u> enter (<u>current</u> leaves) the system; the opposite of an anode.

cathodic protection — A method of preventing oxidation of the exposed metal in structures by imposing a small electrical voltage between the structure and the ground.

Cd — *See* <u>cadmium</u>.

CdTe — *See* <u>cadmium telluride</u>.

cell (battery) — A single unit of an electrochemical device capable of producing direct voltage by converting chemical energy into electrical energy. A battery usually consists of several cells electrically connected together to produce higher voltages. (Sometimes the terms cell and <u>battery</u> are used interchangeably). *See also* <u>photovoltaic (PV) cell</u>.

cell barrier — A very thin region of static electric charge along the interface of the positive and negative layers in a <u>photovoltaic cell</u>. The barrier inhibits the movement of <u>electrons</u> from one layer to the other, so that higher-energy electrons from one side diffuse preferentially through it in one direction, creating a current and thus a <u>voltage</u> across the cell. Also called <u>depletion zone</u> or space charge.

cell junction — The area of immediate contact between two layers (positive and negative) of a **photovoltaic cell**. The junction lies at the center of the **cell barrier** or **depletion zone**.

charge — The process of adding electrical energy to a **battery**.

charge carrier — A free and mobile conduction **electron** or **hole** in a **semiconductor**.

charge controller — A component of a **photovoltaic system** that controls the flow of current to and from the **battery** to protect it from over-charge and over-discharge. The charge controller may also indicate the system operational status.

charge factor — A number representing the time in hours during which a **battery** can be charged at a constant current without damage to the battery. Usually expressed in relation to the total **battery capacity**, i.e., C/5 indicates a charge factor of 5 hours. Related to **charge rate**.

charge rate — The current applied to a **cell** or **battery** to restore its **available capacity**. This rate is commonly normalized by a charge control device with respect to the rated capacity of the **cell** or battery.

chemical vapor deposition (CVD) — A method of depositing **thin semiconductor films** used to make certain types of **photovoltaic devices**. With this method, a **substrate** is exposed to one or more vaporized compounds, one or more of which contain desirable constituents. A chemical reaction is initiated, at or near the substrate surface, to produce the desired material that will condense on the substrate.

cleavage of lateral epitaxial films for transfer (CLEFT) —

A process for making inexpensive gallium arsenide (GaAs) **photovoltaic cells** in which a thin film of GaAs is grown atop a thick, single-crystal GaAs (or other suitable material) **substrate** and then is cleaved from the substrate and incorporated into a cell, allowing the substrate to be reused to grow more thin-film GaAs.

cloud enhancement — The increase in solar intensity caused by reflected **irradiance** from nearby clouds.

combined collector — A **photovoltaic device** or **module** that provides useful heat energy in addition to electricity.

concentrating photovoltaics (CPV) — A solar technology that uses lenses or mirrors to concentrate sunlight onto high-efficiency solar cells.

concentrating solar power (CSP) — A solar technology that use mirrors to reflect and concentrate sunlight onto receivers that convert solar energy to heat. This thermal energy is then used to produce electricity with a steam turbine or heat engine driving a generator.

concentrator — A **photovoltaic module**, which includes optical components such as lenses (**Fresnel lens**) to direct and concentrate sunlight onto a **solar cell** of smaller area. Most concentrator **arrays** must directly face or track the sun. They can increase the power flux of sunlight hundreds of times.

conduction band (or conduction level) — An energy band in a **semiconductor** in which **electrons** can move freely in a solid, producing a net transport of charge.

conductor — The material through which electricity is transmitted, such as an electrical wire, or transmission or distribution line.

contact resistance — The resistance between metallic contacts and the **semiconductor**.

contingency reserves — Reserve services that are sufficient to cover the unplanned trip (disconnect) of a large generator or transmission line and maintain system balance. Contingency reserves are generally split between spinning and non-spinning reserves, and are often based on the largest single hazard (generator or transmission capacity).

conversion efficiency — *See* **photovoltaic (conversion) efficiency**.

converter — A unit that converts a **direct current** (dc) voltage to another dc voltage.

copper indium diselenide (CuInSe2, or CIS) — A **polycrystalline** **thin-film** photovoltaic material (sometimes incorporating **gallium** (CIGS) and/or sulfur).

copper zinc tin sulfide/selenide (CZTS) — A polycrystalline thin-film photovoltaic material.

crystalline silicon — A type of **photovoltaic cell** made from a slice of silicon or **polycrystalline silicon**.

current — *See* **electric current**.

current at maximum power (Imp) — The **current** at which maximum power is available from a **module**.

current-voltage (I-V) curve — *See* **I-V curve**

cutoff voltage — The **voltage** levels (activation) at which the **charge controller** disconnects the **photovoltaic array** from the **battery** or the **load** from the battery.

cycle — The discharge and subsequent charge of a **battery**.

Czochralski process — A method of growing large size, high quality **semiconductor** crystal by slowly lifting a seed crystal from a molten bath of the material under careful cooling conditions.

D

dangling bonds — A chemical bond associated with an atom on the surface layer of a crystal. The bond does not join with another atom of the crystal, but extends in the direction of exterior of the surface.

days of storage — The number of consecutive days the **stand-alone system** will meet a defined **load** without solar energy input. This term is related to system availability.

DC — *See* **direct current**.

DC-to-DC converter — Electronic circuit to convert **direct current voltage**s (e.g., photovoltaic module **voltage**) into other levels (e.g., **load voltage**). Can be part of a **maximum power point tracker**.

deep-cycle battery — A battery with large plates that can withstand many discharges to a low **state-of-charge**.

deep discharge — Discharging a battery to 20% or less of its full charge capacity.

defect — *See* **light-induced defects**

demand response — The process of using voluntary load reductions during peak hours.

depth of discharge (DOD) — The **ampere-hours** removed

from a fully charged **cell** or **battery**, expressed as a percentage of rated capacity. For example, the removal of 25 ampere-hours from a fully charged 100 ampere-hours rated cell results in a 25% depth of discharge. Under certain conditions, such as discharge rates lower than that used to rate the cell, depth of discharge can exceed 100%.

dendrite — A slender threadlike spike of pure crystalline material, such as **silicon**.

dendritic web technique — A method for making sheets of **polycrystalline silicon** in which silicon **dendrites** are slowly withdrawn from a melt of silicon whereupon a web of silicon forms between the dendrites and solidifies as it rises from the melt and cools.

depletion zone — Same as **cell barrier**. The term derives from the fact that this microscopically thin region is depleted of **charge carriers** (free **electrons** and **hole**).

design month — The month having the combination of **insolation** and **load** that requires the maximum energy from the **photovoltaic array**.

diffuse insolation — Sunlight received indirectly as a result of scattering due to clouds, fog, haze, dust, or other obstructions in the atmosphere. Opposite of **direct insolation**.

diffuse radiation — Radiation received from the sun after reflection and scattering by the atmosphere and ground.

diffusion furnace — Furnace used to make junctions in **semiconductor**s by diffusing dopant atoms into the surface of the material.

diffusion length — The mean distance a free **electron** or **hole** moves before recombining with another hole or electron.

diode — An electronic device that allows current to flow in one direction only. *See also* blocking **diode** and **bypass diode**.

direct beam radiation — Radiation received by direct solar rays. Measured by a pyrheliometer with a solar aperture of 5.7° to transcribe the solar disc.

direct current (DC) — A type of electricity transmission and distribution by which electricity flows in one direction through the **conductor**, usually relatively low **voltage** and high current. To be used for typical 120 volt or 220 **volt** household appliances, DC must be converted to **alternating current**, its opposite.

direct insolation — Sunlight falling directly upon a collector. Opposite of **diffuse insolation**.

discharge — The withdrawal of electrical energy from a **battery**.

discharge factor — A number equivalent to the time in hours during which a battery is discharged at constant current usually expressed as a percentage of the total battery capacity, i.e., C/5 indicates a discharge factor of 5 hours. Related to **discharge rate**.

discharge rate — The rate, usually expressed in **amperes** or time, at which current is taken from the **battery**.

disconnect — Switch gear used to connect or disconnect components in a **photovoltaic system**.

dispatching (economic dispatch) — A method by which system operators decide how much output should be scheduled from plants.

distributed energy resources (DER) — A variety of small, modular power-generating technologies that can be combined with energy management and storage systems and used to improve the operation of the electricity delivery system, whether or not those technologies are connected to an electricity grid.

distributed generation — A popular term for localized or on-site power generation.

distributed power — Generic term for any power supply located near the point where the power is used. Opposite of central power. *See also* **stand-alone systems**.

distributed systems — Systems that are installed at or near the location where the electricity is used, as opposed to central systems that supply electricity to **grids**. A residential **photovoltaic system** is a distributed system.

donor — In a **photovoltaic device**, an **n-type dopant**, such as **phosphorus**, that puts an additional **electron** into an energy level very near the **conduction band**; this electron is easily exited into the conduction band where it increases the electrical conductivity over than of an undoped **semiconductor**.

donor level — The level that donates **conduction electrons** to the system.

dopant — A chemical element (impurity) added in small amounts to an otherwise pure semiconductor material to modify the electrical properties of the material. An n-dopant introduces more electrons. A p-dopant creates electron vacancies (**holes**).

doping — The addition of **dopants** to a **semiconductor**.

downtime — Time when the photovoltaic system cannot provide power for the **load**. Usually expressed in hours per year or that percentage.

dry cell — A **cell** (battery) with a captive **electrolyte**. A primary battery that cannot be recharged.

duty cycle — The ratio of active time to total time. Used to describe the operating regime of appliances or loads in **photovoltaic systems**.

duty rating — The amount of time an **inverter** (power conditioning unit) can produce at full rated power.

E

edge-defined film-fed growth (EFG) — A method for making sheets of **polycrystalline silicon** for **photovoltaic devices** in which molten silicon is drawn upward by capillary action through a mold.

electric circuit — The path followed by electrons from a power source (generator or battery), through an electrical system, and returning to the source.

electric current — The flow of electrical energy (electricity) in a **conductor**, measured in **amperes**.

electrical grid — An integrated system of electricity distribution, usually covering a large area.

electricity — Energy resulting from the flow of charge particles, such as **electrons** or **ions**.

electrochemical cell — A device containing two conducting **electrodes**, one positive and the other negative, made of dissimilar materials (usually metals) that are immersed in a chemical solution (**electrolyte**) that transmits positive **ions** from the negative to the positive electrode and thus forms an electrical charge. One or more cells constitute a **battery**.

electrode — A conductor that is brought in conducting contact with a ground.

electrodeposition — Electrolytic process in which a metal is deposited at the **cathode** from a solution of its ions.

electrolyte — A nonmetallic (liquid or solid) conductor that carries **current** by the movement of **ions** (instead of **electrons**) with the liberation of matter at the **electrodes** of an **electrochemical cell**.

electron — An elementary particle of an atom with a negative electrical charge and a mass of 1/1837 of a proton; electrons surround the positively charged nucleus of an atom and determine the chemical properties of an atom. The movement of electrons in an electrical **conductor** constitutes an electric **current**.

electron hole pair — The result of light of sufficient energy dislodging an electron from its bond in a crystal, which creates a hole. The free electron (negative charge) and the hole (positive charge) are a pair. These pairs are the constituents of electricity.

electron volt (eV) — The amount of kinetic energy gained by an electron when accelerated through an electric potential difference of 1 Volt; equivalent to 1.603×10^{-19}; a unit of energy or work.

energy — The capability of doing work; different forms of energy can be converted to other forms, but the total amount of energy remains the same.

energy audit — A survey that shows how much energy used in a home, which helps find ways to use less energy.

energy contribution potential — **Recombination** occurring in the emitter region of a **photovoltaic cell**.

energy density — The ratio of available energy per pound; usually used to compare storage **batteries**.

energy imbalance service — A market service that provides for the management of unscheduled deviations in individual generator output or load consumption.

energy levels — The energy represented by an **electron** in the band model of a substance.

epitaxial growth — The growth of one crystal on the surface of another crystal. The growth of the deposited crystal is oriented by the **lattice** structure of the original crystal.

equalization — The process of restoring all **cells** in a **battery** to an equal **state-of-charge**. Some battery types may require a complete discharge as a part of the equalization process.

equalization charge — The process of mixing the **electrolyte** in batteries by periodically overcharging the batteries for a short time.

equalizing charge — A continuation of normal **battery** charging, at a **voltage** level slightly higher than the normal end-of-charge voltage, in order to provide cell **equalization** within a battery.

equinox — The two times of the year when the sun crosses the equator and night and day are of equal length; occurring around March 20 or 21 (spring equinox) and September 22 or 23 (fall equinox).

exciton — A quasi-particle created in a semiconductor that is composed of an **electron hole pair** in a bound state. An exciton can be generated by and converted back into a **photon**.

external quantum efficiency (external QE or EQE) — **Quantum efficiency** that includes the effect of optical losses, such as transmission through the cell and reflection of light away from the cell.

extrinsic semiconductor — The product of **doping** a pure **semiconductor**.

F

Fermi level — Energy level at which the probability of finding an **electron** is one-half. In a metal, the Fermi level is very near the top of the filled levels in the partially filled **valence band**. In a **semiconductor**, the Fermi level is in the **band gap**.

fill factor — The ratio of a **photovoltaic cell**'s actual power to its power if both current and **voltage** were at their maxima. A key characteristic in evaluating cell performance.

fixed tilt array — A **photovoltaic array** set in at a fixed angle with respect to horizontal.

flat-plate array — A **photovoltaic (PV) array** that consists of non-concentrating **PV modules**.

flat-plate module — An arrangement of **photovoltaic cell**s or material mounted on a rigid flat surface with the cells exposed freely to incoming sunlight.

flat-plate photovoltaics (PV) — A PV array or module that consists of nonconcentrating elements. Flat-plate **arrays** and **modules** use direct and diffuse sunlight, but if the array is fixed in position, some portion of the direct sunlight is lost because of oblique sun-angles in relation to the array.

float charge — The **voltage** required to counteract the **self-discharge** of the **battery** at a certain temperature.

float life — The number of years that a **battery** can keep its stated capacity when it is kept at float charge.

float service — A battery operation in which the battery is normally connected to an external current source; for instance, a battery charger which supplies the battery load< under normal conditions, while also providing enough energy input to the battery to make up for its internal quiescent losses, thus keeping the battery always up to full power and ready for service.

float-zone process — In reference to solar photovoltaic cell manufacture, a method of growing a large-size, high-quality crystal whereby coils heat a **polycrystalline** ingot placed atop a single-crystal seed. As the coils are slowly raised the molten interface beneath the coils becomes single crystal.

frequency — The number of repetitions per unit time of a complete waveform, expressed in Hertz (Hz).

frequency regulation — This indicates the variability in the output **frequency**. Some loads will switch off or not operate properly if frequency variations exceed 1%.

Fresnel lens — An optical device that focuses light like a magnifying glass; concentric rings are faced at slightly different angles so that light falling on any ring is focused to the same point.

full sun — The amount of power density in sunlight received at the earth's surface at noon on a clear day (about 1,000 Watts/square meter).

G

Ga — *See* **gallium**.

GaAs — *See* **gallium arsenide**.

gallium (Ga) — A chemical element, metallic in nature, used in making certain kinds of solar cells and **semiconductor** devices.

gallium arsenide (GaAs) — A crystalline, high-efficiency compound used to make certain types of **solar cells** and **semiconductor** material.

gassing — The evolution of gas from one or more of the **electrodes** in the **cells** of a **battery**. Gassing commonly results from local action **self-discharge** or from the electrolysis of water in the **electrolyte** during charging.

gassing current — The portion of charge **current** that goes into electrolytical production of hydrogen and oxygen from the electrolytic liquid. This current increases with increasing **voltage** and temperature.

gel-type battery — Lead-acid **battery** in which the **electrolyte** is composed of a silica gel matrix.

gigawatt (GW) — A unit of power equal to 1 billion Watts; 1 million kilowatts, or 1,000 megawatts.

grid — *See* **electrical grid**.

grid-connected system — A solar electric or **photovoltaic (PV) system** in which the **PV array** acts like a central generating plant, supplying power to the **grid**.

grid-interactive system — Same as **grid-connected system**.

grid lines — Metallic contacts fused to the surface of the **solar cell** to provide a low resistance path for **electrons** to flow out to the cell interconnect wires.

H

harmonic content — The number of frequencies in the output **waveform** in addition to the primary **frequency** (50 or 60 Hz.). Energy in these harmonic frequencies is lost and may cause excessive heating of the **load**.

heterojunction — A region of electrical contact between two different materials.

high voltage disconnect — The **voltage** at which a **charge controller** will disconnect the **photovoltaic array** from the batteries to prevent overcharging.

high voltage disconnect hysteresis — The **voltage** difference between the **high voltage disconnect** set point and the voltage at which the full **photovoltaic array current** will be reapplied.

hole — The vacancy where an electron would normally exist in a solid; behaves like a positively charged particle.

homojunction — The region between an n-layer and a p-layer in a single material, photovoltaic cell.

hybrid system — A solar electric or **photovoltaic system** that includes other sources of electricity generation, such as wind or diesel generators.

hydrogenated amorphous silicon — **Amorphous silicon** with a small amount of incorporated hydrogen. The hydrogen neutralizes dangling bonds in the amorphous silicon, allowing **charge carriers** to flow more freely.

I

incident light — Light that shines onto the face of a **solar cell** or **module**.

independent system operator (ISO) — The entity responsible for maintaining system balance, reliability, and electricity market operation.

indium oxide — A wide band gap **semiconductor** that can be heavily **doped** with tin to make a highly conductive, transparent **thin film**. Often used as a front contact or one component of a **heterojunction** solar cell.

infrared radiation — Electromagnetic radiation whose wavelengths lie in the range from 0.75 micrometer to 1000 micrometers; invisible long wavelength radiation (heat) capable of producing a thermal or **photovoltaic effect**, though less effective than visible light.

ingot — A casting of material, usually crystalline silicon, from which slices or wafers can be cut for use in a solar cell.

input voltage — This is determined by the total power required by the current loads and the voltage of any **direct**

current loads. Generally, the larger the **load**, the higher the inverter input **voltage**. This keeps the **current** at levels where switches and other components are readily available.

insolation — The solar power density incident on a surface of stated area and orientation, usually expressed as **Watts** per square meter or **Btu** per square foot per hour. *See also***diffuse insolation** and **direct insolation**.

interconnect — A **conductor** within a **module** or other means of connection that provides an electrical interconnection between the **solar cells**.

internal quantum efficiency (internal QE or IQE) — A type of **quantum efficiency**. Refers to the efficiency with which light not transmitted through or reflected away from the cell can generate **charge carriers** that can generate current.

intrinsic layer — A layer of **semiconductor** material, used in a **photovoltaic device**, whose properties are essentially those of the pure, undoped, material.

intrinsic semiconductor — An undoped **semiconductor**.

inverted metamorphic multijunction (IMM) cell — A photovoltaic cell that is a multijunction device whose layers of semiconductors are grown upside down. This special manufacturing process yields an ultra-light and flexible cell that also converts solar energy with high efficiency.

inverter — A device that converts **direct current** electricity to **alternating current** either for stand-alone systems or to supply power to an electricity grid.

ion — An electrically charged atom or group of atoms that has lost or gained **electrons**; a loss makes the resulting particle positively charged; a gain makes the particle negatively charged.

irradiance — The direct, diffuse, and reflected solar radiation that strikes a surface. Usually expressed in **kilowatts** per square meter. Irradiance multiplied by time equals **insolation**.

ISPRA guidelines — Guidelines for the assessment of **photovoltaic** power plants, published by the Joint Research Centre of the Commission of the European Communities, Ispra, Italy.

i-type semiconductor — **Semiconductor** material that is left intrinsic, or undoped so that the concentration of charge carriers is characteristic of the material itself rather than of added impurities.

I-V curve — A graphical presentation of the current versus the voltage from a photovoltaic device as the load is increased from the short circuit (no load) condition to the open circuit (maximum voltage) condition. The shape of the curve characterizes cell performance.

J

joule — A metric unit of energy or work; 1 joule per second equals 1 **watt** or 0.737 foot-pounds; 1 **Btu** equals 1,055 joules.

junction — A region of transition between **semiconductor** layers, such as a p/n junction, which goes from a region that has a high concentration of acceptors (p-type) to one that has a high concentration of donors (n-type).

junction box — A **photovoltaic** (PV) generator junction box is an enclosure on the module where PV strings are electrically connected and where protection devices can be located, if necessary.

junction diode — A **semiconductor** device with a junction and a built-in potential that passes current better in one direction than the other. All **solar cells** are junction **diodes**.

K

kerf— The width of a cut used to create **wafers** from silicon ingots, often resulting in the loss of semiconductor material.

kilowatt (kW) — A standard unit of electrical power equal to 1000 **watts**, or to the energy consumption at a rate of 1000 **joules** per second.

kilowatt-hour (kWh) — 1,000 thousand watts acting over a period of 1 hour. The kWh is a unit of energy. 1 kWh=3600 kJ.

L

langley (L) — Unit of solar **irradiance**. One gram calorie per square centimeter. 1 L = 85.93 kwh/m2.

lattice — The regular periodic arrangement of atoms or molecules in a crystal of semiconductor material.

lead-acid battery — A general category that includes batteries with plates made of pure lead, lead-antimony, or lead-calcium immersed in an acid electrolyte.

levelized cost of energy (LCOE) — The cost of energy of a solar system that is based on the system's installed price, its total lifetime cost, and its lifetime electricity production.

life — The period during which a system is capable of operating above a specified performance level.

life-cycle cost — The estimated cost of owning and operating a **photovoltaic system** for the period of its useful life.

light-induced defects — Defects, such as **dangling bonds**, induced in an **amorphous silicon** semiconductor upon initial exposure to light.

light trapping — The trapping of light inside a semiconductor material by refracting and reflecting the light at critical angles; trapped light will travel further in the material, greatly increasing the probability of absorption and hence of producing charge carriers.

line-commutated inverter — An inverter that is tied to a power **grid** or line. The commutation of power (conversion from **direct current** to **alternating current**) is controlled by the power line, so that, if there is a failure in the power grid, the **photovoltaic system** cannot feed power into the line.

liquid electrolyte battery — A battery containing a liquid solution of acid and water. Distilled water may be added to these batteries to replenish the **electrolyte** as necessary. Also called a flooded battery because the plates are covered with the electrolyte.

load — The demand on an energy producing system; the energy consumption or requirement of a piece or group of equipment. Usually expressed in terms of **amperes** or **watts** in reference to electricity.

load circuit — The wire, switches, fuses, etc. that connect the **load** to the power source.

load current (A) — The current required by the electrical device.

load forecast — Predictions of future demand. For normal operations, daily and weekly forecasts of the hour-by-hour demand are used to help develop generation schedules to ensure that sufficient quantities and types of generation are available when needed.

load resistance — The resistance presented by the load. *See also* **resistance**.

locational marginal price (LMP) — The price of a unit of energy at a particular electrical location at a given time. LMPs are influenced by the nearby generation, load level, and transmission constraints and losses.

low voltage cutoff (LVC) — The **voltage** level at which a **charge controller** will disconnect the **load** from the **battery**.

low voltage disconnect — The **voltage** at which a **charge controller** will disconnect the load from the batteries to prevent over-discharging.

low voltage disconnect hysteresis — The **voltage** difference between the low voltage disconnect set point and the voltage at which the **load** will be reconnected.

low voltage warning — A warning buzzer or light that indicates the low battery **voltage** set point has been reached.

M

maintenance-free battery — A sealed **battery** to which water cannot be added to maintain **electrolyte** level.

majority carrier — Current carriers (either free **electrons** or **holes**) that are in excess in a specific layer of a **semiconductor** material (electrons in the n-layer, holes in the p-layer) of a **cell**.

maximum power point (MPP) — The point on the current-voltage (**I-V**) curve of a module under illumination, where the product of **current** and **voltage** is maximum. For a typical silicon cell, this is at about 0.45 volts.

maximum power point tracker (MPPT) — Means of a power conditioning unit that automatically operates the photovoltaic generator at its **maximum power point** under all conditions.

maximum power tracking — Operating a **photovoltaic array** at the **peak power point** of the array's **I-V curve** where maximum power is obtained. Also called peak power tracking.

measurement and characterization — A field of research that involves assessing the characteristics of photovoltaic materials and devices.

megawatt (MW) — 1,000 **kilowatts**, or 1 million **watts**; standard measure of electric power plant generating capacity.

megawatt-hour — 1,000 **kilowatt-hours** or 1 million **watt-hours**.

metrology — The science of measurement.

microgroove — A small groove scribed into the surface of a **solar cell**, which is filled with metal for contacts.

micrometer (micron) — One millionth of a meter.

minority carrier — A current carrier, either an **electron** or a **hole**, that is in the minority in a specific layer of a **semiconductor** material; the diffusion of minority carriers under the action of the cell **junction** **voltage** is the **current** in a **photovoltaic device**.

minority carrier lifetime — The average time a **minority carrier** exists before **recombination**.

modified sine wave — A **waveform** that has at least three states (i.e., positive, off, and negative). Has less **harmonic content** than a square wave.

modularity — The use of multiple **inverters** connected in parallel to service different loads.

module — *See* **photovoltaic (PV) module**.

module derate factor — A factor that lowers the **photovoltaic module current** to account for field operating conditions such as dirt accumulation on the module.

monolithic — Fabricated as a single structure.

movistor — Short for metal oxide varistor. Used to protect electronic circuits from surge currents such as those produced by lightning.

multicrystalline — A **semiconductor** (photovoltaic) material composed of variously oriented, small, individual crystals. Sometimes referred to as polycrystalline or semicrystalline.

multijunction device — A high-efficiency **photovoltaic device** containing two or more cell **junctions**, each of which is optimized for a particular part of the **solar spectrum**.

multi-stage controller — A **charging controller** unit that allows different charging

currents as the battery nears full state_of_charge.

N

nanometer — One billionth of a meter.

National Electrical Code (NEC) — Contains guidelines for all types of electrical installations. The 1984 and later editions of the NEC contain Article 690, "Solar Photovoltaic Systems" which should be followed when installing a PV system.

National Electrical Manufacturers Association (NEMA) — This organization sets standards for some non-electronic products like junction boxes.

NEC — *See* **National Electrical Code**.

NEMA — *See* **National Electrical Manufacturers Association**.

nickel cadmium battery — A battery containing nickel and cadmium plates and an alkaline **electrolyte**.

nominal voltage — A reference **voltage** used to describe **batteries**, **modules**, or systems (i.e., a 12-volt or 24-volt battery, module, or system).

normal operating cell temperature (NOCT) — The

estimated temperature of a **photovoltaic module** when operating under 800 w/m2 **irradiance**, 20°C **ambient temperature** and wind speed of 1 meter per second. NOCT is used to estimate the nominal operating temperature of a module in its working environment.

n-type — Negative **semiconductor** material in which there are more **electrons** than **holes**; **current** is carried through it by the flow of **electrons**.

n-type semiconductor — A **semiconductor** produced by **doping** an **intrinsic semiconductor** with an **electron-donor** impurity (e.g., **phosphorus** in **silicon**).

n-type silicon — **Silicon** material that has been **doped** with a material that has more **electrons** in its atomic structure than does silicon.

O

ohm — A measure of the electrical resistance of a material equal to the resistance of a circuit in which the potential difference of 1 volt produces a current of 1 ampere.

one-axis tracking — A system capable of rotating about one axis.

open-circuit voltage (Voc) — The maximum possible voltage across a photovoltaic cell; the voltage across the cell in sunlight when no current is flowing.

operating point — The **current** and **voltage** that a photovoltaic **module** or **array** produces when connected to a **load**. The operating point is dependent on the load or the batteries connected to the output terminals of the array.

orientation — Placement with respect to the cardinal directions, N, S, E, W; **azimuth** is the measure of orientation from north.

outgas — *See* **gassing**.

overcharge — Forcing **current** into a fully charged **battery**. The battery will be damaged if overcharged for a long period.

P

packing factor — The ratio of **array** area to actual land area or building envelope area for a system; or, the ratio of total **solar cell** area to the total **module** area, for a module.

panel — *See* **photovoltaic (PV) panel**.

parallel connection — A way of joining **solar cells** or **photovoltaic modules** by connecting positive leads together and negative leads together; such a configuration increases the **current**, but not the **voltage**.

passivation — A chemical reaction that eliminates the detrimental effect of electrically reactive atoms on a **solar cell's** surface.

peak demand/load — The maximum energy demand or load in a specified time period.

peak power current — Amperes produced by a photovoltaic **module** or **array** operating at the **voltage** of the **I-V curve** that will produce maximum power from the module.

peak power point — Operating point of the **I-V (current-**

voltage) curve for a **solar cell** or **photovoltaic module** where the product of the current value times the **voltage** value is a maximum.

peak power tracking — *See* **maximum power tracking**.

peak sun hours — The equivalent number of hours per day when solar **irradiance** averages 1,000 w/m2. For example, six peak sun hours means that the energy received during total daylight hours equals the energy that would have been received had the irradiance for six hours been 1,000 w/m2.

peak watt — A unit used to rate the performance of **solar cells**, **modules**, or **arrays**; the maximum nominal output of a **photovoltaic device**, in **watts** (Wp) under standardized test conditions, usually 1,000 watts per square meter of sunlight with other conditions, such as temperature specified.

phosphorous (P) — A chemical element used as a **dopant** in making semiconductor layers.

photocurrent — An electric current induced by radiant energy.

photoelectric cell — A device for measuring light intensity that works by converting light falling on, or reach it, to electricity, and then measuring the current; used in photometers.

photoelectrochemical cell — A type of **photovoltaic device** in which the electricity induced in the cell is used immediately within the cell to produce a chemical, such as hydrogen, which can then be withdrawn for use.

photon — A particle of light that acts as an individual unit of energy.

photovoltaic(s) (PV) — Pertaining to the direct conversion of light into electricity.

photovoltaic (PV) array — An interconnected system of PV **modules** that function as a single electricity-producing unit. The modules are assembled as a discrete structure, with common support or mounting. In smaller systems, an array can consist of a single module.

photovoltaic (PV) cell — The smallest semiconductor element within a PV **module** to perform the immediate conversion of light into electrical energy (**direct current voltage** and **current**). Also called a solar cell.

photovoltaic (PV) conversion efficiency — The ratio of the electric power produced by a photovoltaic device to the power of the sunlight incident on the device.

photovoltaic (PV) device — A solid-state electrical device that converts light directly into **direct current** electricity of voltage-current characteristics that are a function of the characteristics of the light source and the materials in and design of the device. Solar photovoltaic devices are made of various **semiconductor** materials including **silicon**, **cadmium sulfide**, **cadmium telluride**, and **gallium arsenide**, and in single crystalline, **multicrystalline**, or amorphous forms.

photovoltaic (PV) effect — The phenomenon that occurs when **photons**, the "particles" in a beam of light, knock **electrons** loose from the atoms they strike. When this property of light is combined with the properties of **semiconductor**s, electrons flow in one direction across a **junction**, setting up a **voltage**. With the addition of circuitry, current will flow and electric power will be available.

photovoltaic (PV) generator — The total of all PV strings of a PV power supply system, which are electrically interconnected.

photovoltaic (PV) module — The smallest environmentally protected, essentially planar assembly of solar cells and ancillary parts, such as interconnections, terminals, (and protective devices such as **diodes**) intended to generate **direct current** power under unconcentrated sunlight. The structural (**load** carrying) member of a module can either be the top layer (superstrate) or the back layer (**substrate**).

photovoltaic (PV) panel — often used interchangeably with PV **module** (especially in one-module systems), but more accurately used to refer to a physically connected collection of modules (i.e., a laminate string of modules used to achieve a required **voltage** and **current**).

photovoltaic (PV) system — A complete set of components for converting sunlight into electricity by the **photovoltaic** process, including the **array** and system components.

photovoltaic-thermal (PV/T) system — A photovoltaic system that, in addition to converting sunlight into electricity, collects the residual heat energy and delivers both heat and electricity in usable form. Also called a total energy system or solar thermal system.

physical vapor deposition — A method of depositing **thin semiconductor photovoltaic films**. With this method, physical processes, such as thermal evaporation or bombardment of ions, are used to deposit elemental **semiconductor** material on a **substrate**.

P-I-N — A semiconductor **photovoltaic (PV)**

device structure that layers an intrinsic semiconductor between a p-type semiconductor and an **n-type semiconductor**; this structure is most often used with **amorphous silicon** PV devices.

plates — A metal plate, usually lead or lead compound, immersed in the **electrolyte** in a **battery**.

plug-and-play PV system — A commercial, off-the-shelf photovoltaic system that is fully inclusive with little need for individual customization. The system can be installed without special training and using few tools. The homeowner plugs the system into a PV-ready circuit and an automatic PV discovery process initiates communication between the system and the utility. The system and grid are automatically configured for optimal operation.

P/N — A **semiconductor photovoltaic device** structure in which the **junction** is formed between a p-type layer and an n-type layer.

pocket plate — A plate for a **battery** in which active materials are held in a perforated metal pocket.

point-contact cell — A high efficiency **silicon** photovoltaic **concentrator** cell that employs light trapping techniques and point-diffused contacts on the rear surface for current collection.

polycrystalline — *See* **multicrystalline**.

polycrystalline silicon — A material used to make **photovoltaic cell**s, which consist of many crystals unlike **single-crystal silicon**.

polycrystalline thin film — A thin film made of **multicrystalline** material.

power — The amount of electrical energy available for doing work, measured in horsepower, Watts, or Btu per hour.

power conditioning — The process of modifying the characteristics of electrical power (for e.g., inverting **direct current** to **alternating current**).

power conditioning equipment — Electrical equipment, or power electronics, used to convert power from a **photovoltaic array** into a form suitable for subsequent use. A collective term for **inverter**, converter, battery charge regulator, and **blocking diode**.

power conversion efficiency — The ratio of output power to input power of the **inverter**.

power density — The ratio of the power available from a battery to its mass (W/kg) or volume (W/l).

power factor (PF) — The ratio of actual power being used in a circuit, expressed in **watts** or **kilowatts**, to the power that is apparently being drawn from a power source, expressed in volt-amperes or kilovolt-amperes.

primary battery — A **battery** whose initial **capacity** cannot be restored by charging.

projected area — The net south-facing glazing area projected on a vertical plane.

p-type semiconductor — A semiconductor in which **holes** carry the current; produced by **doping** an **intrinsic semiconductor** with an **electron acceptor** impurity (e.g., **boron** in **silicon**).

pulse-width-modulated (PWM) wave inverter — A type of power **inverter** that produce a high quality (nearly sinusoidal) voltage, at minimum current harmonics.

PV — *See* **photovoltaic(s)**.

pyranometer — An instrument used for measuring global solar **irradiance**.

pyrheliometer — An instrument used for measuring **direct beam** solar **irradiance**. Uses an aperture of 5.7° to transcribe the solar disc.

Q

quad — One quadrillion **Btu** (1,000,000,000,000,000 Btu).

qualification test — A procedure applied to a selected set of **photovoltaic modules** involving the application of defined electrical, mechanical, or thermal stress in a prescribed manner and amount. Test results are subject to a list of defined requirements.

quantum efficiency (QE) — The ratio of the number of **charge carriers** collected by a photovoltaic cell to the number of **photons** of a given energy shining on the cell. Quantum efficiency relates to the response of a solar cell to the different wavelengths in the spectrum of light shining on the cell. QE is given as a function of either wavelength or energy. Optimally, a solar cell should generate considerable electrical current for wavelengths that are most abundant in sunlight.

R

ramp — A change in generation output.

ramp rate — The ability of a generating unit to change its output over some unit of time, often measured in MW/min.

Rankine cycle — A thermodynamic cycle used in steam turbines to convert heat energy into work. **Concentrating solar power** plants often rely on the Rankine cycle. In CSP systems, mirrors focus sunlight on a heat-transfer fluid. This is used to creates steam, which spins a turbine to generate electricity.

rated battery capacity — The term used by battery manufacturers to indicate the maximum amount of energy that can be withdrawn from a battery under specified discharge rate and temperature. *See also* **battery capacity**.

rated module current (A) — The current output of a **photovoltaic module** measured at **standard test conditions** of 1,000 w/m2 and 25°C cell temperature.

rated power — Rated power of the **inverter**. However, some units can not produce rated power continuously. *See also* **duty rating**.

reactive power — The sine of the phase angle between the **current** and **voltage** waveforms in an **alternating current** system. *See also* **power factor**.

recombination — The action of a free electron falling back into a **hole**. Recombination processes are either radiative, where the energy of recombination results in the emission of a photon, or nonradiative, where the energy of recombination is given to a second electron which then relaxes back to its original energy by emitting phonons. Recombination can take place in the bulk of the semiconductor, at the surfaces, in the junction region, at defects, or between interfaces.

rectifier — A device that converts **alternating current** to **direct current**. *See also* **inverter**.

regulator — Prevents overcharging of batteries by controlling charge cycle-usually adjustable to conform to specific battery needs.

remote systems — *See* **stand-alone systems**.

reserve capacity — The amount of generating capacity a central power system must maintain to meet **peak loads**.

resistance (R) — The property of a **conductor**, which opposes the flow of an **electric current** resulting in the generation of heat in the conducting material. The measure of the resistance of a given conductor is the electromotive force needed for a unit current flow. The unit of resistance is **ohms**.

resistive voltage drop — The voltage developed across a **cell** by the **current** flow through the resistance of the cell.

reverse current protection — Any method of preventing unwanted **current** flow from the battery to the **photovoltaic array** (usually at night). *See also* **blocking diode**.

ribbon (photovoltaic) cells — A type of **photovoltaic device** made in a continuous process of pulling material from a molten bath of photovoltaic material, such as **silicon**, to form a thin sheet of material.

RMS — *See* **root mean square**.

root mean square (RMS) — The square root of the average square of the instantaneous values of an ac output. For a sine wave the RMS value is 0.707 times the peak value. The equivalent value of **alternating current**, I, that will produce the same heating in a **conductor** with resistance, R, as a dc current of value I.

S

sacrificial anode — A piece of metal buried near a structure that is to be protected from corrosion. The metal of the sacrificial **anode** is intended to corrode and reduce the corrosion of the protected structure.

satellite power system (SPS) — Concept for providing large amounts of electricity for use on the Earth from one or more satellites in geosynchronous Earth orbit. A very large array of solar cells on each satellite would provide electricity, which would be converted to microwave energy and beamed to a receiving antenna on the ground. There, it would be reconverted into electricity and distributed the same as any other centrally generated power, through a grid.

scheduling — The general practice of ensuring that a generator is committed and available when needed. It also can refer to scheduling of imports or exports of energy into or out of a **balancing area**.

Schottky barrier — A **cell barrier** established as the interface between a **semiconductor**, such as **silicon**, and a sheet of metal.

scribing — The cutting of a grid pattern of grooves in a semiconductor material, generally for the purpose of making interconnections.

sealed battery — A battery with a captive electrolyte and a resealing vent cap, also called a valve-regulated battery. Electrolyte cannot be added.

seasonal depth of discharge — An adjustment factor used in some system sizing procedures which "allows" the battery to be gradually discharged over a 30-90 day period of poor solar **insolation**. This factor results in a slightly smaller **photovoltaic array**.

secondary battery — A **battery** that can be recharged.

self-discharge — The rate at which a **battery**, without a **load**, will lose its charge.

semiconductor — Any material that has a limited capacity for conducting an electric current. Certain semiconductors, including **silicon**, **gallium   arsenide**, **copper   indium diselenide**, and **cadmium telluride**, are uniquely suited to the **photovoltaic** conversion process.

semicrystalline — *See* **multicrystalline**.

series connection — A way of joining **photovoltaic cell**s by connecting positive leads to negative leads; such a configuration increases the **voltage**.

series controller — A **charge controller** that interrupts the charging current by open-circuiting the **photovoltaic (PV) array**. The control element is in series with the PV array and **battery**.

series regulator — Type of **battery** charge regulator where the charging **current** is controlled by a switch connected in series with the photovoltaic **module** or **array**.

series resistance — Parasitic resistance to **current** flow in a **cell** due to mechanisms such as resistance from the bulk of the **semiconductor** material,   metallic   contacts,   and interconnections.

shallow-cycle battery — A battery with small plates that cannot withstand many discharges to a low state-of-charge.

shelf life of batteries — The length of time, under specified conditions, that a **battery** can be stored so that it keeps its guaranteed capacity.

short-circuit current (Isc) — The **current** flowing freely through an external circuit that has no **load** or resistance; the maximum current possible.

shunt controller — A **charge controller** that redirects or shunts the charging current away from the battery. The controller requires a large heat sink to dissipate the current from the short-circuited **photovoltaic array**. Most shunt controllers are for smaller systems producing 30 **amperes** or less.

shunt regulator — Type of a **battery** charge regulator where the charging current is controlled by a switch connected in parallel with the **photovoltaic (PV) generator**. Shorting the PV generator prevents overcharging of the battery.

Siemens process — A commercial method of making purified **silicon**.

silicon (Si) — A semi-metallic chemical element that makes an excellent semiconductor material for **photovoltaic devices**. It crystallizes in face-centered cubic **lattice** like a diamond. It's commonly found in sand and quartz (as the oxide).

sine wave — A **waveform** corresponding to a single-frequency periodic oscillation that can be mathematically represented as a function of amplitude versus angle in which the value of the curve at any point is equal to the sine of that angle.

sine wave inverter — An inverter that produces utility-quality, **sine wave** power forms.

single-crystal material — A material that is composed of a single crystal or a few large crystals.

single-crystal silicon — Material with a single crystalline formation. Many **photovoltaic cell**s are made from single-crystal silicon.

single-stage controller — A **charge controller** that redirects all charging current as the battery nears full **state-of-charge**.

smart grid — An intelligent electric power system that regulates the two-way flow of electricity and information between power plants and consumers to control grid activity.

soft costs — Non-hardware costs related to PV systems, such as financing, permitting, installation, interconnection, and inspection.

solar cell — *See* **photovoltaic (PV) cell**.

solar constant — The average amount of solar radiation that reaches the earth's upper atmosphere on a surface perpendicular to the sun's rays; equal to 1353 watts per square meter or 492 Btu per square foot.

solar cooling — The use of solar thermal energy or solar electricity to power a cooling appliance. **Photovoltaic systems** can power evaporative coolers ("swamp" coolers), heat-pumps, and air conditioners.

solar energy — Electromagnetic energy transmitted from the sun (solar radiation). The amount that reaches the earth is equal to one billionth of total solar energy generated, or the equivalent of about 420 trillion kilowatt-hours.

solar-grade silicon — Intermediate-grade **silicon** used in the manufacture of **solar cells**. Less expensive than electronic-grade silicon.

solar insolation — *See* **insolation**.

solar irradiance — *See* **irradiance**.

solar noon — The time of the day, at a specific location, when the sun reaches its highest, apparent point in the sky.

solar panel — *See* **photovoltaic (PV) panel**.

solar resource — The amount of solar **insolation** a site receives, usually measured in kWh/m2/day, which is equivalent to the number of **peak sun hours**.

solar spectrum — The total distribution of electromagnetic radiation emanating from the sun. The different regions of the solar spectrum are described by their wavelength range. The visible region extends from about 390 to 780 nanometers (a nanometer is one billionth of one meter). About 99 percent of solar radiation is contained in a wavelength region from 300 nm (ultraviolet) to 3,000 nm (near-infrared). The combined radiation in the wavelength region from 280 nm to 4,000 nm is called the broadband, or total, solar radiation.

solar thermal electric systems — Solar energy conversion technologies that convert solar energy to electricity, by heating a working fluid to power a turbine that drives a generator. Examples of these systems include central receiver systems, parabolic dish, and solar trough.

space charge — *See* **cell barrier**.

specific gravity — The ratio of the weight of the solution to the weight of an equal volume of water at a specified temperature. Used as an indicator of battery **state-of-**

charge.

spinning reserve — Electric power plant or utility capacity on-line and running at low power in excess of actual **load**.

split-spectrum cell — A compound **photovoltaic device** in which sunlight is first divided into spectral regions by optical means. Each region is then directed to a different cell optimized for converting that portion of the spectrum into electricity. Such a device achieves significantly greater overall conversion of incident sunlight into electricity. *See also* **mulitjunction device**.

sputtering — A process used to apply photovoltaic **semiconductor** material to a **substrate** by a **physical vapor deposition** process where high-energy **ions** are used to bombard elemental sources of semiconductor material, which eject vapors of atoms that are then deposited in thin layers on a **substrate**.

square wave — A **waveform** that has only two states, (i.e., positive or negative). A square wave contains a large number of harmonics.

square wave inverter — A type of inverter that produces **square wave** output. It consists of a **direct current** source, four switches, and the **load**. The switches are power **semiconductor**s that can carry a large **current** and withstand a high **voltage** rating. The switches are turned on and off at a correct sequence, at a certain frequency.

Staebler-Wronski effect — The tendency of the sunlight to electricity conversion efficiency of **amorphous silicon photovoltaic device**s to degrade (drop) upon initial exposure to light.

stand-alone system — An autonomous or **hybrid**

photovoltaic system not connected to a **grid**. May or may not have storage, but most stand-alone systems require **batteries** or some other form of storage.

standard reporting conditions (SRC) — A fixed set of conditions (including meteorological) to which the electrical performance data of a **photovoltaic module** are translated from the set of actual test conditions.

standard test conditions (STC) — Conditions under which a **module** is typically tested in a laboratory.

standby current — This is the amount of current (power) used by the **inverter** when no load is active (lost power). The efficiency of the inverter is lowest when the load demand is low.

stand-off mounting — Technique for mounting a **photovoltaic array** on a sloped roof, which involves mounting the **modules** a short distance above the pitched roof and tilting them to the optimum angle.

starved electrolyte cell — A **battery** containing little or no free fluid **electrolyte**.

state-of-charge (SOC) — The available capacity remaining in the **battery**, expressed as a percentage of the rated capacity.

storage battery — A device capable of transforming energy from electric to chemical form and vice versa. The reactions are almost completely reversible. During discharge, chemical energy is converted to electric energy and is consumed in an external circuit or apparatus.

stratification — A condition that occurs when the acid concentration varies from top to bottom in the battery **electrolyte**. Periodic, controlled charging at **voltage**s that produce **gassing** will mix the electrolyte. *See also* **equalization**.

string — A number of photovoltaic **modules** or **panels** interconnected electrically in series to produce the operating **voltage** required by the **load**.

sub-hourly energy markets — Electricity markets that operate on time steps of 5 minutes. Approximately 60% of all electricity in the United States is currently traded in sub-hourly markets, running at 5-minute intervals so that maximum flexibility can be obtained from the generation fleet.

substrate — The physical material upon which a **photovoltaic cell** is applied.

subsystem — Any one of several components in a photovoltaic system (i.e., **array**, controller, **batteries**, **inverter**, **load**).

sulfation — A condition that afflicts unused and discharged **batteries**; large crystals of lead sulfate grow on the plate, instead of the usual tiny crystals, making the battery extremely difficult to recharge.

superconducting magnetic energy storage (SMES) — SMES technology uses the superconducting characteristics of low-temperature materials to produce intense magnetic fields to store energy. It has been proposed as a storage option to support large-scale use of **photovoltaics** as a means to smooth out fluctuations in power generation.

superconductivity — The abrupt and large increase in electrical conductivity exhibited by some metals as the temperature approaches absolute zero.

superstrate — The covering on the sunny side of a **photovoltaic (PV) module**, providing protection for the PV materials from impact and environmental degradation while allowing maximum transmission of the appropriate wavelengths of the solar spectrum.

surge capacity — The maximum power, usually 3-5 times the rated power, that can be provided over a short time.

system availability — The percentage of time (usually expressed in hours per year) when a **photovoltaic system** will be able to fully meet the **load** demand.

system operating voltage — The **photovoltaic array** output **voltage** under **load**. The system operating voltage is dependent on the load or batteries connected to the output terminals.

system storage — *See* **battery capacity**.

T

tare loss — Loss caused by a **charge controller**. One minus tare loss, expressed as a percentage, is equal to the controller efficiency.

temperature compensation — A circuit that adjusts the **charge controller** activation points depending on battery temperature. This feature is recommended if the battery temperature is expected to vary more than ±5°C from **ambient temperature**.

temperature factors — It is common for three elements in **photovoltaic system** sizing to have distinct temperature corrections: a factor used to decrease **battery capacity** at cold temperatures; a factor used to decrease **PV**

module voltage at high temperatures; and a factor used to decrease the **current** carrying capability of wire at high temperatures.

thermophotovoltaic cell (TPV) — A device where sunlight concentrated onto a absorber heats it to a high temperature, and the thermal radiation emitted by the absorber is used as the energy source for a **photovoltaic cell** that is designed to maximize **conversion efficiency** at the wavelength of the thermal radiation.

thick-crystalline materials — Semiconductor material, typically measuring from 200-400 microns thick, that is cut from ingots or ribbons.

thin film — A layer of **semiconductor** material, such as **copper indium diselenide** or **gallium arsenide**, a few microns or less in thickness, used to make **photovoltaic cell**s.

thin film photovoltaic module — A **photovoltaic module** constructed with sequential layers of **thin film** semiconductor materials. *See also* **amorphous silicon**.

tilt angle — The angle at which a **photovoltaic array** is set to face the sun relative to a horizontal position. The tilt angle can be set or adjusted to maximize seasonal or annual energy collection.

tin oxide — A wide band-gap **semiconductor** similar to **indium oxide**; used in **heterojunction** solar cells or to make a transparent conductive film, called NESA glass when deposited on glass.

total AC load demand — The sum of the **alternating current** loads. This value is important when selecting an **inverter**.

total harmonic distortion — The measure of closeness in shape between a waveform and its fundamental component.

total internal reflection — The trapping of light by refraction and reflection at critical angles inside a semiconductor device so that it cannot escape the device and must be eventually absorbed by the semiconductor.

tracking array — A **photovoltaic (PV) array** that follows the path of the sun to maximize the solar radiation incident on the PV surface. The two most common orientations are (1) one axis where the array tracks the sun east to west and (2) two-axis tracking where the array points directly at the sun at all times. Tracking arrays use both the direct and diffuse sunlight. Two-axis tracking arrays capture the maximum possible daily energy.

transformer — An electromagnetic device that changes the **voltage** of **alternating current** electricity.

transparent conducting oxide (TCO) — A doped metal oxide used to coat and improve the performance of optoelectronic devices such as photovoltaics and flat panel displays. Most TCO films are fabricated with polycrystalline or amorphous microstructures and are deposited on glass. The current industry-standard TCO is indium tin oxide. Indium is relatively rare and expensive, so research is ongoing to develop improved TCOs based on alternative materials.

tray cable (TC) - may be used for interconnecting **balance-of-systems**.

trickle charge — A charge at a low rate, balancing through **self-discharge** losses, to maintain a

tunneling — Quantum mechanical concept whereby an **electron** is found on the opposite side of an insulating barrier without having passed through or around the barrier.

cell or **battery** in a fully charged condition.

two-axis tracking — A **photovoltaic array** tracking system capable of rotating independently about two axes (e.g., vertical and horizontal).

U

ultraviolet — Electromagnetic radiation in the wavelength range of 4 to 400 nanometers.

underground feeder (UF) — May be used for **photovoltaic array** wiring if sunlight resistant coating is specified; can be used for interconnecting **balance-of-system** components but not recommended for use within battery enclosures.

underground service entrance (USE) — May be used within battery enclosures and for interconnecting **balance-of-systems**.

uninterruptible power supply (UPS) — The designation of a power supply providing continuous uninterruptible service. The UPS will contain **batteries**.

utility-interactive inverter — An **inverter** that can function only when tied to the utility **grid**, and uses the prevailing line-voltage frequency on the utility line as a control parameter to ensure that the photovoltaic system's output is fully synchronized with the utility power.

V

vacuum evaporation - The deposition of **thin films** of **semiconductor** material by the evaporation of elemental sources in a vacuum.

vacuum zero — The energy of an **electron** at rest in empty space; used as a reference level in energy band diagrams.

valence band — The highest energy band in a **semiconductor** that can be filled with **electrons**.

valence level energy/valence state — Energy content of an **electron** in orbit about an atomic nucleus. Also called bound state.

varistor — A voltage-dependent variable resistor. Normally used to protect sensitive equipment from power spikes or lightning strikes by shunting the energy to ground.

vented cell — A **battery** designed with a vent mechanism to expel gases generated during charging.

vertical multijunction (VMJ) cell — A compound cell made of different **semiconductor** materials in layers, one above the other. Sunlight entering the top passes through successive cell barriers, each of which converts a separate portion of the spectrum into electricity, thus achieving greater total conversion efficiency of the incident light. Also called a multiple junction cell. *See also* **multijunction device** and **split-spectrum cell**.

volt (V) — A unit of electrical force equal to that amount of electromotive force that will cause a steady **current** of one **ampere** to flow through a resistance of one **ohm**.

voltage — The amount of electromotive force, measured

in **volts**, that exists between two points.

voltage at maximum power (Vmp) — The **voltage** at which maximum power is available from a **photovoltaic module**.

voltage protection — Many **inverters** have sensing circuits that will disconnect the unit from the battery if input **voltage** limits are exceeded.

voltage regulation — This indicates the variability in the output **voltage**. Some **loads** will not tolerate voltage variations greater than a few percent.

W

wafer — A thin sheet of **semiconductor** (photovoltaic material) made by cutting it from a single crystal or ingot.

watt — The rate of energy transfer equivalent to one **ampere** under an electrical pressure of one **volt**. One watt equals 1/746 horsepower, or one **joule** per second. It is the product of **voltage** and **current** (amperage).

waveform — The shape of the phase power at a certain frequency and amplitude.

wet shelf life — The period of time that a charged **battery**, when filled with **electrolyte**, can remain unused before dropping below a specified level of performance.

window — A wide **band gap** material chosen for its transparency to light. Generally used as the top layer of a **photovoltaic device**, the window allows almost all of the light to reach the **semiconductor** layers beneath.

wire types — *See* Article 300 of <u>**National Electric Code**</u> for more information.

work function — The energy difference between the <u>**Fermi level**</u> and <u>**vacuum zero**</u>. The minimum amount of energy it takes to remove an <u>**electron**</u> from a substance into the vacuum.

Z

zenith angle — the angle between the direction of interest (of the sun, for example) and the zenith (directly overhead).

*This glossary is reprinted from https://energy.gov/eere/sunshot/solar-energy-glossary and is not included in the copyrighted material of this book.

About the Author

 **Nicholas Gorden** is the CEO of Shine Solar, LLC, a solar panel installation company co-founded with his brother, Caleb Gorden, in Bentonville, Arkansas. Shine Solar was born at the exact right time that "going solar" finally made sense — all the necessary elements were happening at the same time: decreased panel costs, increased efficiency, generous tax credits and incentives, and newly available solar financing options.

Nicholas thinks that the coolest thing about solar panels is that they just sit on your roof make power as long as the sun is shining. Aside from this savvy observation, he has made it one of his goals to share the good news that it is finally time to go solar — not just because it is good for the environment, but because it is a sound financial practice and a good investment.

As an expert in gauging consumer needs and saving homeowners' money, Shine Solar was created when Nicholas saw an opportunity in the Midwest to deliver a less expensive option to homeowners for their energy needs. Shine Solar recently opened a second office in Springfield, Missouri, in order to service the increasing demand for saving money with solar panel installations.

According to Nicholas, although the coolest thing about solar panels is that they just sit on your roof and make power, the coolest thing about him is his family. But, unlike solar panels, Nicholas's family doesn't just sit around. The

Gorden family is always on the move — snowboarding down a mountain or swimming, snorkeling, or wakeboarding through the water. Nicholas credits his wife and family for making him look really good and for supporting his endeavors, as well as his business partners and mentors who have shared their life experiences and provided insight and counsel.

You can find Nicholas and his Shine Solar team on Facebook at facebook.com/Shinesolarpower/ or at their website at www.shinesolar.com. Of course, old-fashioned calling works, too. Call 1-844-80-SHINE to speak with a professional.